365

POSITIVE VIBES

~ 365 ~

365

365

POSITIVE VIBES

~ 365 ~

ONE YEAR OF POSITIVITY

PRESTON MITCHUM JR.

365

Positive Vibes 365, One Year of Positivity
© Copyright 2024 Preston Mitchum Jr

ISBN: 978-1-956581-51-5
ISBN: 978-1-956581-54-6 HB

Scripture quotations marked NIV are taken from the Holy Bible, New International Version, Copyright © 1973, 1978, 1984, 2011 by Biblica, Inc. Used by permission of Zondervan. All rights reserved worldwide. The "NIV" and "New International Version" are trademarks registered in the United States Patent and Trademark Office by Biblica, Inc.

ERIN GO BRAGH Publishing

Canyon Lake, Texas
www.ErinGoBraghPublishing.com

365

INTRODUCTION

No matter what is going on around author Preston Mitchum, Jr., he is always looking for that positive perspective on the situation. He celebrates the good times and looks for ways to learn through the tough ones. In this new book, his message remains:

Positive Thoughts, Positive Vibes.

Having received such incredible feedback from his ever-increasing number of readers and social media followers, Preston put pen to paper once again to bring you even more positivity in our ever-changing world.

Whether you read these messages back-to-back, or every once in a while, the goal is to help boost your perception of life, take

time to appreciate it and find the positives that are all around us.

God has given us such an amazing gift - this life. Let's show our appreciation for it by cherishing each and every moment.

Positive thinking isn't about ignoring life's difficulties—it's about finding strength in adversity, seeking solutions instead of dwelling on problems, and believing that brighter days are ahead. Every thought, no matter how small, has the power to influence our emotions and actions.

365

JANUARY 1ST

The start of a new year is a powerful moment, offering us the chance to reflect on the wonderful experiences and growth we've had over the past year. It's also a time to look inward, to consider the changes we want to make, and the improvements we strive for in our lives. This is your fresh start—a blank page for new goals, new dreams, and the opportunity to shape your present and future into what you envision. As we step into this new chapter, let's keep moving forward together, embracing the Positive Vibes movement. May we continue to encourage, inspire, and uplift one another on this incredible journey we call life.

365

JANUARY 2ND

Start each day by letting your inner light shine. A genuine smile can bring about positive energy and that energy can have a powerful impact on those around you.

Nourish your spirit by surrounding yourself with people who lift you up and help your light shine.

Embrace your unique self and let your happiness attract all of the good things that this life has to offer.

POSITIVE THOUGHTS, POSITIVE VIBES!

JANUARY 3<u>RD</u>

Today and every day, you should be extremely proud of yourself. Smile at the person you see in the mirror and embrace the many changes you've gone through.

You are stronger, wiser, than you were yesterday. You have the ability to do anything you set your mind to.

Don't be afraid to challenge yourself and to strive to be the best possible version of yourself every day.

POSITIVE THOUGHTS, POSITIVE VIBES!

365

JANUARY 4TH

I see you rising each morning, pushing forward, and giving your best to the world. I understand that things aren't always easy, and challenges can seem overwhelming. When making changes or taking leaps feels difficult, remember to take a step back and look at your supportive tribe.

The people around you can provide the inspiration and encouragement you need. Surrounding yourself with positive and motivating individuals is key to becoming the best version of yourself.

POSITIVE THOUGHTS, POSITIVE VIBES!

365

JANUARY 5TH

I woke up this morning grateful for another day and the endless possibilities ahead. As we continue to grow and focus on maintaining a positive mindset, seeking out the good can ignite that positive energy within you.

Hopefully, this light will shine bright and positively impact those around you. Soak up the sunshine, my friends, and let your light shine bright.

POSITIVE THOUGHTS, POSITIVE VIBES!

365

JANUARY 6TH

NATIONAL CUDDLE DAY

There are moments in life when a simple hug or cuddle can make all the difference. On National Cuddle Day, take the opportunity to snuggle up with someone special and embrace the positive energy they bring. Cuddling offers a chance for your mind, body, and soul to relax, inviting a deep sense of peace and connection.

POSITIVE THOUGHTS, POSITIVE VIBES!

365

JANUARY 7TH

Thank you for joining us in this Positive Vibes movement! Did you know we have daily affirmation books for kids as well? They are designed to inspire and encourage our young people. They deserve some positivity in their lives as well.

We invite all educators, community organizations, mom groups, daycares, school libraries, and anyone working with children to reach out to us.

Let's work together to put these books into the hands of our youth and add another positive tool to their journey through life.

365

JANUARY 8TH

We live in a world filled with negativity. I often find myself asking people to share something good because shifting our focus to positive events can create a meaningful change in our perspective.

It's essential to highlight the good in order to minimize the negativity around us. Surrounding ourselves with positive individuals can help foster a more balanced and uplifting atmosphere.

365

JANUARY 9TH

I woke up this morning and I am grateful for my amazing friends who support and encourage me every day.

Mr. Rogers said it best "look for the helpers today." I choose to be a helper and offer a helping hand to someone in need. Working together we can achieve some amazing things and make the world a better place.

POSITIVE THOUGHTS, POSITIVE VIBES!

365

JANUARY 10TH

Remember to keep shining brightly, smiling, and letting your light positively impact the world around you. Sometimes, the smallest gestures—a kind word, a warm smile, or a heartfelt hug—can make all the difference in someone's life.

Take a moment today, and every day, to offer a little kindness. Together, we can spread love and compassion, making the world a better and brighter place for everyone. Keep shining, and never underestimate the power of your light!

365

JANUARY 11TH

Together, we are working to create the change we wish to see in the world. Each day, we have the opportunity to bring a bit of positivity into the world and make a difference in someone's life. The impact of that comes back to us, allowing us to reflect on the things that bring happiness and positivity into our own lives.

As we continue to grow and evolve, the light within us will shine even brighter, adding more positivity to the world. Keep being the beautiful soul that you are—your unique essence is exactly what the world needs.

JANUARY 12TH

Treasure the beautiful people in your life who fill your soul with joy.

Make sure that they are aware of your appreciation and love for them just as they are. Whether during the good or tough times, true friends will consistently support you. It is indeed a blessing to be surrounded by positive, uplifting people who inspire you to reach your fullest potential.

POSITIVE THOUGHTS, POSITIVE VIBES!

365

JANUARY 13TH

I can't help but reflect on the amazing people in my life who continue to inspire and encourage me to be the best version of myself. These are the individuals with whom I have deep, invigorating conversations, and after spending time with them, I leave feeling even more energized than before.

My third book, Positive Vibes: Fireside Thoughts, is dedicated to those who ignite the spark that fuels the fire within me, driving my passion to make a lasting impact in the lives of others.

365

JANUARY 14TH

In order for a fresh start, the mind, body and soul need cleansing. The song sung by Shirley Caesar said it best, "Lord if you find anything that is not like you, take it away."

Ask God to participate in your clearing promise. My oldest son, Carter, says often, God with another "o" is good. So, if God is good why not add him to the process. A fresh start is not an easy task but having as much good as possible in the mix will help. Move forward, mix in good people, and let God order your steps. If it's not good, ask him to take it away!

365

JANUARY 15TH

How do we free ourselves from hate and anger? Both can eat away at our soul and not allow us to move forward. They say you must forgive, but sometimes you just don't know how. Forgive and not forget?

Today is the day you take control of how you view the situation. You can forgive, so you can move forward. It's in the past for a reason and now you live in the present. Smile at the hate and laugh at the anger. Your positivity will overcome negativity any day.

JANUARY 16<u>TH</u>

We all have the ability to spread a little sunshine and bring joy into someone's life.

Whether it's through a kind word, a hug, or simply sharing a smile, these small gestures can truly make a difference.

Let's continue this movement of positive vibes, keeping each other inspired.

POSITIVE THOUGHTS, POSITIVE VIBES!

365

JANUARY 17TH

Change your attitude and change your life. Debbie Downer should not be hanging around for long. Life is waiting for you to live it, but what if your attitude stinks? Why are you unhappy? What things need to change to get you on the right path? Well, your chance of getting there starts with your attitude.

Allow your attitude to take you places that you have never been before. Allow it to attract the people you want in your life. Anything is possible with the right outlook on life. It's time to make the change!

365

JANUARY 18ᵀᴴ

You know when something isn't right. When it doesn't feel right, and you know you need a change. Believe in yourself enough to know that you can make yourself a priority and know you are worth it. You are worthy of feeling proud of yourself. You are worthy of knowing you deserve wonderful things. Stop settling for less. Stand up for you and allow yourself the grace to understand that it may be difficult but it's worth it. Also, give yourself the grace to know it takes time. You don't change your life overnight, but every day you can make progress in creating a whole new you.

365

JANUARY 19TH

Take a moment to reflect on the people in your life who allow you to be fully yourself. The ones whose presence feels like nourishment for your soul. Their openness and vulnerability create space for everyone to grow.

Many of us are on a journey to become the best version of ourselves, and having the right people around you helps you evolve and let your beautiful light shine even brighter. Keep smiling, keep shining, and continue spreading those positive vibes!

365

JANUARY 20ᵀᴴ

Remember, today and every day, to prioritize the things that bring balance and harmony to your life. In a world that constantly pushes us to keep going, we often forget to pause and reflect on what we truly need to feel centered. It's essential to surround yourself with positivity whether through uplifting people, joyful activities, or simply moments of peace.

Sometimes, it's okay to say 'no' to the demands around you so you can say 'yes' to self-care and personal growth. Strive to be the best version of yourself, because the world needs your unique light to shine at its brightest!

365

JANUARY 21ST

Incorporating daily affirmations into your routine is a powerful way to cultivate balance and positivity in your life. Our "Positive Vibes" books are filled with uplifting insights and motivational nuggets designed to reinforce a positive mindset, helping you navigate the inevitable challenges we all face.

Whether you're seeking to elevate your own day or inspire someone else, grab a copy today—it's a gift that keeps on giving. Share the positivity with a friend and watch how a little encouragement can make a big difference.

JANUARY 22ND

You have questions but no one seems to have the answers. It's just life! Sometimes life can be full of questions with very few answers. You muddled through some days just trying to figure things out. Why me? When will it end? Where should I go and to whom can I turn?

God might have the answers or at least a place of rest while you figure things out. Life will throw you a few curve balls, but God can help you hit one right out of the park. It might just have to be on His time and terms. Be patient and wait for the right pitch before you swing. That ball is coming.

365

JANUARY 23ᴿᴰ

Optimism is a superpower that brings hope and confidence, even in uncertain times.

Like Julie Bates, we can shine a light for ourselves and others, inspiring everyone to push toward brighter possibilities.

Take a moment today to reflect on your unique gift and how it can make a difference.

I AM OPTIMISTIC THAT
YOU CAN DO THIS!

POSITIVE THOUGHTS, POSITIVE VIBES!

365

JANUARY 24ᵀᴴ

NATIONAL PEANUT BUTTER DAY

To all the peanut butter lovers, today is the perfect day to savor a spoonful of your favorite treat. Whether you're crafting a classic peanut butter and jelly sandwich or baking something sweet, indulge in the rich, comforting flavor of peanut butter. Why? Because peanut butter can help boost your energy level, reduce the risk of heart disease and many more benefits. Of course, if you are allergic to peanuts, there are alternatives that are just as delectable. So, savor it. On National Peanut Butter Day, allow yourself to enjoy the simple sweetness it brings!

365

JANUARY 25TH

Many of us spend time pondering what our next move should be. Often, we wait for every detail to align perfectly before we act. The truth is, the perfect moment to make a change or take a leap is right now. Waiting too long can lead to missed opportunities.

Don't delay; seize the chance to create the change you desire and find the happiness you seek in life.

POSITIVE THOUGHTS, POSITIVE VIBES!

365

JANUARY 26TH

The road traveled is often filled with detours, potholes, and a few necessary pit stops. No matter how challenging the journey becomes, it's essential to persevere because there is always a light at the end of the tunnel.

Life may lead us through tough times and make us stumble, but remember that trouble is only temporary. It's important to love yourself, find strength within, and embrace those positive vibes to celebrate the good times when they come to you.

365

JANUARY 27TH

Take a look in the mirror; what do you see? Our personal experiences shape how we view ourselves. Do you like what you see? Are you happy with the person you are? Today is the day you accept yourself, love who you are, and try to embrace the changes you need to make in your life.

Bit by bit, piece by piece, you will continue to shape the person in the mirror. Looking into the mirror gives you a chance to reflect within.

Love who you are because we all have something positive to share.

365

JANUARY 28TH

GOOD MORNING, EVERYONE!

Sometimes life takes us on an unexpected yet welcomed path. Blessings come when you least expect it. Embrace Gods path.

It was designed for you and you only!

Today when you find yourself on a path that seems unexpected, take a deep breath, smile, and take a step towards your future.

YOU CAN DO THIS!

POSITIVE THOUGHTS, POSITIVE VIBES!

365

JANUARY 29TH

It was just a simple gaze that sparked the connection. Our eyes met for a split second. My attention was focused on you when you noticed my gaze. They say "the Gaze" is a powerful element of social interaction. What was the emotional effect? What role did the gaze play in our social connection? It was an opportunity to allow your inner spirit to be vulnerable to what 'could be'. Look into my eyes and witness the things I see, feel and want. A simple gaze in the right direction could be exactly what the doctor ordered. Enjoy the Positive Vibes flowing through you and the power of the gaze someone has to offer.

365

JANUARY 30TH

Most of us wake up each day with a seemingly endless to-do list, making it feel nearly impossible to find balance amidst the chaos. In the midst of all that needs to be accomplished, carving out time for personal growth and change can seem overwhelming. However, it's crucial to dedicate at least a few moments each day to activities that bring peace and stillness to your mind, body, and soul. This quiet time isn't just about getting through the tasks at hand—it's about replenishing your spirit, nourishing your soul, and ensuring you have the inner strength to face whatever comes your way.

365

JANUARY 31ˢᵀ

You know some of us out there cannot hide how we feel. It's written all over your face. The energy you exude can tell me it's not a good day. You're having a hard time seeing all the good things around you because that one thing has you stuck.

I'm here to find that smile of yours so you can wear it as you get through this one. It's time to sing a new song, move those two left feet and understand you got this. You don't want to be here living in the midst of sadness, not when there is joy right around the corner. Time is precious so push aside the negative and allow the positive to change what's on your face.

365

FEBRUARY 1ST

In our life time we will come across false promises. People will make promises that they cannot or choose not to keep.

How important is it to keep your promise? Is your word your bond? Sometimes we make the mistakes of making promises when we just need to keep it real.

Don't stress about making everyone happy. Superheroes are not needed all the time. The only promise you need to keep is giving your best.

POSITIVE THOUGHTS, POSITIVE VIBES!

365

FEBRUARY 2ND

GROUNDHOG DAY

It's that day when we wake up wondering will the groundhog see sunshine or will he see his shadow?

Groundhog Day reveals if we'll have six more weeks of winter or if spring is just around the corner, helping us plan for the season ahead. Just like in life, we plant good seeds, hopeful for the arrival of spring and the chance to watch our efforts bloom.

FEBRUARY 3<u>RD</u>

The moment I walked into the room, I felt the positive energy flowing. There's something special about being surrounded by like-minded people who view life with optimism.

Together, we can analyze challenges and find solutions that help us keep moving forward. Engaging in inspiring and encouraging conversations sets our minds in the right place to face whatever comes our way.

When you enter a space with the right energy, you're bound to leave with a positive mindset.

365

FEBRUARY 4ᵀᴴ

The power of a smile is truly remarkable! By sharing your smile with others, you can spread positivity and brighten someone's day without even realizing it. Surround yourself with people who bring you joy and laughter, and keep that wonderful glow shining from within.

Share your lovely smile and let it bring
a little happiness to others!

POSITIVE THOUGHTS, POSITIVE VIBES!

365

FEBRUARY 5TH

I love the song 'God's Grace' by Reverend Luther Barnes. On those tough days when you're not sure if things are going to pan out, remember that you've made it this far because of the grace of God.

There's a resilient spirit inside of you that keeps persevering and moving forward. Yes, you've conquered tough times before, and even when others may have doubted you, here you are, standing strong. You've come this far, and you will keep progressing towards becoming the best version of yourself.

FEBRUARY 6TH

Let your light shine brightly, radiating a positive energy that touches and uplifts everyone you encounter. Each of us carries a unique inner spark, a force that, when nurtured, has the power to transform the world in a way only we can. Embrace that power within you and let it guide your actions, knowing that your energy is a gift to the world.

Continue striving to become the best version of yourself—not just for your own growth, but to inspire and elevate those around you.

365

FEBRUARY 7ᵀᴴ

There are moments when we pause and feel the urge to create the change we wish to see in ourselves and the world around us. This journey begins by looking within—focusing on the small, subtle shifts we desire. As we cultivate self-awareness and embrace growth, we naturally begin to shape the energy, relationships, and experiences that surround us.

It's often said that we attract the energy we radiate. So, as we continue to invest in our personal growth, we will draw in more positive, uplifting, and empowering forces.

365

FEBRUARY 8TH

At the end of the day, it's essential to make choices that align with what's right. Life will bring us many different situations, some of which will challenge us, but staying true to what's right is key. And it's not just about doing what's right for ourselves, but also for others. Deep down, your intuition will guide you toward the right path, nudging you toward the choices that matter most. Sometimes, doing the right thing may not feel comfortable in the moment, but trust that the reward is far greater than any temporary discomfort. In the end, you'll feel fulfilled and proud, knowing that you stood by your values.

365

FEBRUARY 9TH

NATIONAL PIZZA DAY

Whether it's one slice, two, or the whole pie, who doesn't love a good pizza—especially on National Pizza Day! If you haven't had a slice in a while, today's the perfect excuse to indulge in that special sauce, melty cheese, and all your favorite toppings. Sharing a pizza with family and friends is sure to bring plenty of laughs and great memories.

Enjoy a slice today, maybe even one tomorrow—but remember, everything in moderation!

365

FEBRUARY 10TH

NATIONAL UMBRELLA DAY

Even when the sky is dark and the rain is pouring down, an umbrella offers the perfect bit of coverage and comfort. It's become an essential tool, ready to shield us during downpours or dreary days. Whether it's bright and colorful or simple and compact, most of us keep an umbrella close by—just in case.

In life, too, we can all use a little extra support and shelter to help us weather the storm during challenging times.

365

FEBRUARY 11TH

NATIONAL MAKE A FRIEND DAY

Friendship is one of life's greatest gifts—it starts with a stranger, and then something magical develops.

On National Make a New Friend Day, why not strike up a conversation with someone in the grocery store, at the gym, or as you pass by on the street? You never know what might happen—that stranger could become one of your closest friends.

Heck, find my page on Facebook and click follow. I love making new friends.

365

FEBRUARY 12TH

It looks like you're ready to love again. You've made yourself a priority, surrounded by good people and things are aligning in the right direction. Change can create the much-needed shift in how you look at things, giving you the right mindset ready for love. Not gonna repeat the same old patterns that didn't work in the past because the new you won't allow it.

That's right let go of the past, live in the present and watch the positive vibes flow. Accept the good, embrace the change, and keep loving yourself. Being ready to love hasn't ever felt this good!

365

FEBRUARY 13TH

Some of us struggle from loving on the inside and the outside of our bodies. We're wandering around trying to figure out where the love went and how do we love again. Some of that could come from past experiences being hurt, giving too much with very little in return. Breakup, divorce, abandonment can play a major part in how you view and interpret love.

Don't let the past hold you back from what is in the present. Take those experiences as life lessons and work on loving yourself all over again. You might have been broken in the past but keep picking up those pieces and forming that new you.

365

FEBRUARY 14ᵀᴴ

Valentine's Day is a time to indulge in sweet moments and celebrate love, whether it's with chocolates, flowers, or heartfelt gifts for that special someone.

But beyond the tokens of affection, today and every day is an opportunity to show those around you how much they mean to you. Let the people in your life—family, friends, and loved ones—feel deeply appreciated for the positivity they bring and the love they share. Make sure they know how cherished they are, not just today, but always.

Love is a gift we give freely, and the more we share it, the more it grows.

365

FEBRUARY 15ᵀᴴ

Sometimes we want to love, or be loved, but understanding and accepting it can be difficult. It could take that special someone to love you in a way that allows your heart to open up.

Jon B. said it best "you gave me someone to love." Yes, the right person, loving the true you, in turn gives you the opportunity to take a chance on love. And that is beautiful!

POSITIVE THOUGHTS, POSITIVE VIBES!

365

FEBRUARY 16TH

All of us are carrying stuff around. Stuff from our past. Now is the time to clean out that backpack so it doesn't go with you into the future.

Things from the past have shaped you but do not define you. You can learn, embrace and let go of the things that have been weighing you down.

Lighten the load so that your spirit can be free. Freeing your spirit will allow your light to shine and hopefully put the past behind you so you can start living in the here and now.

365

FEBRUARY 17TH

NATIONAL RANDOM ACTS OF KINDNESS DAY

While I like the idea of making this day special, why limit it to just one day? We should be helping share acts of kindness where ever we go.

Could you hold a door open for someone? Reaching for that item on the top shelf for someone shorter? Bending down and picking up something an elderly person dropped? Maybe paying it forward with a cup of coffee or inexpensive meal for someone else. Put a smile on someone's face who wasn't expecting it. Be kind.

365

FEBRUARY 18ᵀᴴ

Look into the eyes and see the soul. You wear your heart on your sleeve. Are you allowing people to feel and experience the true you? They say sometimes you can stand next to a person and feel their spirit. Is it good or bad? Broken or healed?

It's ok to let people in, because you can control how they make you feel. Connection comes through feeling, and feeling allows us to grow. Those experiences of sharing who we are allow us to be at peace. Accepting what we give to the world is pretty darn good. Bring on the good, and heal the broken.

365

FEBRUARY 19TH

We know all about priorities, right?

Priorities can drive us crazy trying to get everything accomplished. Some days it feels like you're losing your marbles. Remember not to let those urgent things crowd the important ones.

Take a moment to breathe and understand what you can and cannot do. Some people travel the world looking for what they need and miss out on what they already have at home. Time will pass you by trying to get everything done so pause and make sure your priorities don't get in the way of living and loving life.

365

FEBRUARY 20TH

Deep down inside is a fear, a fear to live. Fear of the unknown, the things you might hold deep within.

The experiences you go through can create an unsafe place inside your mind. You grasp for things, people and places that will help provide that safe place. Past experiences might be holding you back from becoming the you that you want to be. Trust and have faith that God has a plan for you. He will not let you face more than you can handle.

TODAY IS THE DAY
TO FACE YOUR FEARS.

FEBRUARY 21ST

Sometimes we love so hard that we don't allow enough room - "Room" for the love to grow and manifest into whatever form it will be. Patrice Rushen said it best, "maybe we need just a little room".

One of the major components of truly loving someone is friendship. Allowing time for the friendship to grow will provide the understanding needed for the love to blossom. Let your heart feel with eyes open and your soul ready. That's right, no need to look back at what could have been, allow the time for the connection to flourish. In time it will show itself and enjoy the beauty in whatever form that might be.

365

FEBRUARY 22ND

You know what? Today it's all about You!

Today is the day you will look deep down within and focus on you. Not your friend's problems or issues but the things you want to tweak about yourself.

We all have those little things we want to work on about ourselves. Today is the day. It's ok to tell your friends that it's self-care day and it will just have to wait. Allowing your light to shine brighter is like wearing glory for the world to see.

365

FEBRUARY 23RD

NATIONAL PUPPY DAY

My good friend and publisher Kathleen J. Shields and I penned the book Pawsitive Vibes Dogs as a way to connect the happy-go-lucky, always excited, looking forward to the next adventure, inspirational way that dogs look at life in hopes of connecting their enthusiasm for life with that of our own. Their unconditional love can teach us so much about how to live our own lives.

So on National Puppy Day, take a moment to watch a funny dog video, pet a friendly pooch or pick up a copy of Pawsitive Vibes Dogs to add to your daily reading.

FEBRUARY 24TH

Who or what inspires You? We talk about it often. Who you decide to surround yourself with is key. Who you allow in your space can provide the spark or inspiration you need.

Pause for a second and take in the many things around you that keep you going. Things like reading, medication, exercise and nutrition can really feed your soul. Take care of your mind, body and soul first which will allow for the awakening. You will then be able to really see and feel who or what inspires you.

FEBRUARY 25TH

We all have goals in life. What are yours? Do you know? If not, get out that pen and paper and start writing. Finish school, career change, fall in love, whatever it might be, write it down.

It all starts with making a list and getting things started. Then you will need to put yourself around people who can ignite that fire. It's called inspiration! Putting yourself around inspiring people will help get you going in the right direction. Your goals are possible with the right plan and support. Get yourself a good mix!

365

FEBRUARY 26TH

NATIONAL SET A GOOD EXAMPLE DAY

Setting a good example is essential, especially for our children and the important people in our lives.

As we continue this Positive Vibes movement, we're showing how each of us can build a healthy, positive lifestyle.

On National Set a Good Example Day, let's take this opportunity to demonstrate the positive examples we can set for those around us.

365

FEBRUARY 27ᵀᴴ

It all starts with loving yourself. How the heck do we do that? I mean, in the crazy world we live in, loving yourself can get lost. Love the uniqueness of you and allow that light to shine. God made you in the image he wanted so embrace it my friend.

Think about all of the wonderful things you already offer to the world. Give from your heart, feel from your soul and speak without ill intent. Your ability to love is already there you just need to start from within and appreciate all the awesomeness you have to offer.

You are beautiful on the inside and out.
Believe it, own it and share it!

365

FEBRUARY 28ᵀᴴ

Are you always trying to please others? Do you find yourself getting lost in taking care of everyone else?

Yes, it's good for us to help others but also wise to take care of ourselves. Your spirit must have time to rejuvenate itself in order to handle what life throws at you.

Without a strong self, your ability to help will be limited. Your ability to make the right choices and decisions could be clouded. Let go and let God lead your thoughts and guide your steps. He will help you decipher what you can do and what you should do.

365

FEBRUARY 29TH

LEAP DAY

While it only comes around once every four years, and this year may not have one, it is still a very important day because it gives you one more chance that year to share some positivity with others.

So if it's not leap day for you this year, you could always jump to March 1st – or you could take a moment to make a leap. Jump up. Clap your hands. Or share a smile with another person.

TAKE THE LEAP TO MAKE TODAY
A BETTER DAY FOR ANOTHER.

365

MARCH 1ST

A song by The Moments says, "I found love on a two-way street and lost it on a lonely highway". Love can be found on many different roads or maybe one road with a few pot holes. Have you looked within? Did you truly have Love? Were you complete enough to find the one that would complement you?

Sometimes we need to be in the right place and space to invite the right love in. True love will enhance what you have already presented and allow that to continue its growth. Be patient and fine tune you first.

POSITIVE THOUGHTS, POSITIVE VIBES!

MARCH 2ND

Come on, stop taking things personally. We all have to put our egos aside. Someone's projection could be a reflection on them. You can deflect the negative and find the positive in how you allow it to affect you. You have control on how things make you feel.

Take a step back and understand before you react. If someone is trying to be cruel or harmful, deflect. You know you. Let that be what you feel.

LET YOUR LIGHT SHINE
AND GLARE OUT THE DARKNESS.

365

MARCH 3RD

NATIONAL I WANT YOU TO BE HAPPY DAY

I love that upbeat tune by Pharrell, Happy—
it makes you want to dance, nod your head,
and move to the beat. On National I Want
you to Be Happy Day, let's all groove,
dance, and do things that bring us real joy.

Today and every day, sprinkle in some
positivity and do the things that make you
truly happy. You deserve every bit of that
joy life has to offer!

MARCH 4ᵀᴴ

You did it! You took a step back and with that, now you get it.

The real meaning in life is not what you have but what you don't have. What you can't see because the road ahead is closed.

You need a detour to take you down a path of open mindedness. Being closed minded will keep you from receiving the blessing right in front of you.

You have the power to change how you think and see the world. Pause every once and awhile to see what you might be missing.

365

MARCH 5TH

There is truth in true friendship.

We hear people talk about it all the time. You know what, so-and-so is my true friend. But what accounts for true friendship? What makes a person a true friend? It's the person that highlights the positives and minimizes the negative. Offers a helping hand but doesn't enable you. The one who reaches out to you because being in your presence just makes them feel better. The one that will hold you accountable when needed. It's that feel-good person that needs nothing more than to soak up your good vibes. There is truth in friendship with the ones that make your soul shine.

MARCH 6TH

Here you go again, feeling sorry for yourself. The "woe is me," song is playing loud in the background. Don't wait around for anyone to listen because everyone is feeling it too. You got this! Troubles don't last, this too shall pass.

Take a step back and reapproach the situation. Try to see it differently in hopes of finding some positivity or the silver lining. It's there but sometimes we don't see it because we're not really looking. We're stuck in the, "woe is me." It's time to get up and see your way through this one. You will be surprised at yourself.

MARCH 7TH

The exchange of energy between two people provides the opportunity for one's soul to be touched. Not only physical touch but through emotions it provides that one of kind connection. It's special!

Something that words cannot describe, it's an unspoken profound effect that the two people have for one another. They show up at a significant time in your life and offer a sense of peace like no other. The love is so strong that you adore everything about them. It's all about accepting their flaws, imperfections and everything about them.

365

MARCH 8TH

Hug me baby, hug me tight…

It feels so good to be able to offer up, as well as, to receive a hug. We've been through some tough times, my friends, but it feels great to be able to offer up a hug, a smile, a kind word. I mean so good to be able to get close to one another again.

From the zoom calls, to video chats, now we have the opportunity to offer up a hug, so come on over here and give me a hug!

POSITIVE THOUGHTS, POSITIVE VIBES!

365

MARCH 9TH

I mean come on, who doesn't love live music? Music rejuvenates the mind, body and soul and can take your heart to places it has never been to. Music allows you to be you.

Feel the Positivity that flows through it, as it always makes you feel good. So, jump in the car and go out in search of some live music. I'm looking forward to seeing you somewhere, feeling the vibes of some good sounds.

365

MARCH 10TH

The ability to accept help is not always easy. It is not easy to open up and allow people in. We all have our reasons for it. We tell ourselves, "I can do it all by myself." We don't always know how to ask for help, or have a hard time verbalizing our needs. They say sometimes asking for help can be the hardest thing you can do.

Surround yourself with good people who you can feel comfortable with in your time of need. We all need someone at some point to assist us and yes, it's ok to say, "I need help." By asking for help you start the process of taking care of you. And yes, we all need the best you have to offer.

365

MARCH 11ᵀᴴ

Do you stare fear in the face? You have to look deep within and use your past experience for strength.

It's not easy to do or attempt something you fear. Taking the leap is not easy but the outcome could be worth it.

You will never know what you can do unless you try. Through this process you will find out more about yourself. Build confidence in the old and new you.

365

MARCH 12TH

Stop allowing others to control your thoughts. Think for yourself! Be you and love who you are today and who you are becoming. Surround yourself with people who believe in and love you, for you. If it's not the case for you, then you're not around the right people.

We should be lifting each other up and enhancing each other's lives. People should make you feel good about who you are. Offer constructive criticism without judgment. You can control your surroundings, which means you can control who is in your orbit!

365

MARCH 13TH

NATIONAL GOOD SAMARITAN DAY

Today, let's celebrate the power of kindness, compassion, and selflessness. Every small act of generosity—whether it's helping a neighbor, offering a kind word, or lending a hand—creates ripples of positive change that touch hearts and transform lives.

We all have the ability to make the world a better place, not with grand gestures, but with genuine care and love for those around us. Let's commit to being the light in someone's day, spreading empathy, and lifting others up, one kind act at a time.

365

MARCH 14<u>TH</u>

Don't be afraid to show off your beauty. I see you feeling good about the way you look today. Show it off, walk out of the house with that fresh new glow. That smile of yours has the ability to change someone's day, so wear it.

Why are you hiding? What is keeping you from giving the world your best? Are you listening to others? The ones who are not lifting you up? The ones who are not filling your cup? No more my friend, look for the ones who support your glow, your shine, because it's unique. It's yours so own it, share it, and believe it.

365

MARCH 15TH

There is an old saying that "time heals all wounds". Things have been pretty tough for you, the journey traveled has had some bumps in the road. When you hit rock bottom there is only one way, up.

Sometimes you need to use "time" to give the ability to get through those tough times. You are using your time more wisely and this is the main factor in seeing the change you want to see. In our lifetime we will go through adversity but how we approach it is key. Give yourself time to look within and find what you need, moving forward with more positive vibes flowing.

365

MARCH 16TH

All right now don't you go laughing at me, I like to get comfy. Yes, that's what I call it, getting "Comfy." I can easily post myself up at a restaurant, grab a nice drink, and sit there for hours just relaxing. It's called being at peace with myself.

I call it getting comfy, you might call it something else. Either way, it's that opportunity for us to just 'be' and not allow any noise to distract us. It provides the opportunity to rebalance ourselves. So, make sure you take some time today to get comfy.

365

MARCH 17TH

The words of the Ben E. King song, "Stand By Me" leads me to wonder; can you be that rock for others, can you be that shoulder to lean on? We all need someone who can be there in our time of need. Whether it's your father, mother, sister, brother or friend. It's truly a blessing when you have that rock. The person who stands strong and keeps you upright.

God will send you an angel. Open your eyes and recognize the beauty in it. The energy will put you back on the positive track in life.

Reference: Ben E King song "Stand By Me" from the single released in 1961

365

MARCH 18TH

There's nothing like a good hug from someone with positive energy. It can go through you and make everything ok. I know some of you don't like to be touched. Touch shows that someone cares, so you need to open up and allow that in.

A hug from the right person can make a world of difference. It's an unspoken gesture that offers comfort and makes the soul feel good. You must remember it's very important to take care of your soul. If your inside feels good then your outside will shine. And yes, we all need to see that light of yours shining bright.

MARCH 19TH

Accepting help can seem like an impossible idea. The idea of trusting someone else to be there for you can be overwhelming. If you surround yourself with the right people though, it can be amazing. Embracing those who truly want the best for you can put you on a path to helping you become the greatest version of yourself. Those who truly love you will show they want to be there for you.

It's not transactional, it's about being there for each other. Don't let these people pass you by, because you're too busy not believing in yourself. You're worth it.

365

MARCH 20TH

Thank you for being such an amazing friend. That person I can depend on. Even during the tough times, having that special someone is so important. It's also wonderful when they highlight those good times in your life.

True friendship is all about understanding and respect, allowing each other the space and time to understand one another. Sharing a few words or just being silent, "balance" is the key which helps you understand the differences as well. You get it, it's an unspoken connection.

365

MARCH 21ST

You hear it over and over again, "misery loves company." Well, I'm sorry, I don't want that company. Try avoiding the negative energy. Try avoiding those people and situations if possible. If you can't find a positive outlook then move on to something else.

Negativity can become contagious and the last thing you need is to catch something else. Your life is already fully packed with stuff to do and take care of. Go search for some positive juice today and drink until your cup runs full.

365

MARCH 22ND

You were once in love and now, you are out of love. Your mind, body and soul are in a different place. It's complicated.

The reason it's complicated, you want to share yourself. You want someone to know, like, love and accept the true you. The question is, are you loving yourself first? Some call it self-care, loving yourself so that your true light will shine.

As you continue to love yourself, you will become the best you. Sharing yourself with the right person or persons will get easier.

365

MARCH 23ᴿᴰ

How important are the people you surround yourself with? The right person can see something in you that you don't see in yourself. Put you on a path that you never expected. A friend of mine said " I had a feeling about you" that feeling was something special.

Stepping into the unknown can be scary but with the right people around you, the support will propel you forward. It's time to step out on faith and see what God has in store for you. Recognizing your gifts, honing them, fine tuning them, and once done, sharing them. Sharing those gifts might just give someone else the spark to travel down that unknown pathway.

MARCH 24TH

Make today your day of rest. Some days you feel so tired, you can barely stand. The ability to get through your day and get into bed is the best feeling.

Your body and spirit need time to rest. Without rest, you find yourself spinning in circles without truly accomplishing the tasks at hand. Put a few things aside and take some time to breathe today.

Let your mind relax and fuel your spirit.

POSITIVE THOUGHTS, POSITIVE VIBES!

MARCH 25TH

It doesn't take much to be kind, and the positive, rippling effect of change can benefit one's life. Acts of kindness can make the world a happier place for everyone. They can boost feelings of confidence, being in control, happiness and optimism. They may also encourage others to repeat the good deeds they've experienced themselves – contributing to a more positive community. Sprinkling in those positive vibes is like adding something to a delicious pot of soup. All of the ingredients come together to make something special. Today is your day to add something to your pot and watch, smell and taste the magic of kindness.

365

MARCH 26ᵀᴴ

Your ability to grow comes from surrounding yourself with good people. Like-minded means people who think alike or have the same view point. We also need folks who think differently to challenge the norm.

It's all about balance! Opposites do attract but they find common ground in acceptance. Understanding one another is key to creating peaceful environments. Most people want the best for themselves and by releasing positive energy, you will attract positive people.

365

MARCH 27TH

Its deep, real deep and you can't figure it out. You turn right you turn left. You call your best friend, neighbor you might even have a conversation with the dog, but you just can't figure it out. Something just doesn't feel right and you can't put a finger on it.

Allow God to provide the peace that you need, to minimize the noise, so you can figure out what is going on. There's an old saying, you have a friend in Jesus, and today might be the day you can call upon him to get you through.

365

MARCH 28TH

There is nothing like relaxing next to a nice fire. Grab some twigs or logs, start up the fire pit and then gaze into the stars. When you sit back and stare into the fire, you get away for a little while. Another opportunity has presented itself to breathe.

Yes, summer nights can be muggy, but gaze onto the stars and allow your mind to relax. We all have different ways to relax, understanding what works for you is key. What gives you that moment to see and feel good? Life's problems, and the hustle and bustle of the world will be there when you get back.

365

MARCH 29TH

I'm living my best life now. You know why, because I'm being me. Giving the world the best I have to offer, and not looking back.

You can feel and see my light shine brightly. Allow the energy I'm giving off you, positively inspire you to do the same. Today is the day you start living your best life. It's all right there for the taking. What are you waiting for?

POSITIVE THOUGHTS, POSITIVE VIBES!

365

MARCH 30TH

NATIONAL TAKE A WALK IN THE PARK DAY

Many of you know the song by Otis Redding, "Sitting on the Dock of the Bay," where he sings about taking it easy and watching time go by. If you're not near a dock, maybe you're close to a park. On National Take a Walk in the Park Day, it's the perfect chance to get outside, take a stroll, and let your mind unwind. The calm of being outdoors—especially when you're with a friend, coworker, or family member—might be just what you need to add a bit of positivity to your day.

365

MARCH 31ˢᵀ

I think Fred Hammond said it best "You are the living word." Yes, one of the greatest gifts my mother gave me was introducing me to the living God. No matter the situation, I know I have a friend in Jesus.

I have found myself on many occasions calling his name. He was sent down from glory to be light for us in our time of need, and to rejoice during the happy times. Feeling blessed to call him my friend. His grace allows me to give of myself and shine my light in hopes of inspiring others.

365

APRIL 1ST

Today, let's embrace the power of laughter, play, and a lighthearted spirit. Life may surprise us with unexpected twists, but the best way to face them is with a smile and an open heart.

Remember, humor can turn any challenge into an opportunity for growth, and laughter connects us all. So, be kind, be joyful, and spread a little joy—because the best kind of trick is the one that makes someone's day brighter.

Here's to finding happiness in the unexpected and turning every moment into a reason to laugh!

365

APRIL 2ᴺᴰ

If you think most things are terrible or just not your cup of tea you may need to look within. Terrible is all in the mind. It's all how you view it or take it in.

Stop looking for the negative and find a little good. Nothing is perfect and some things will just be downright awful. Today, you have the power to change your perspective and perception. It's all in your mind and it's time to allow your heart to step in. Use a combination of mind, body and soul and see the positivity shine through.

365

APRIL 3RD

I am all about people-watching. I love sitting back and watching the body language, the way people laugh, the way people look at each other... You can really collect some positive energy from watching people.

To be honest it just feels good to be able to be in the midst of people, to have those experiences. So why not soak it in? Why not take a sit back, grab a beverage and do a little people-watching?

POSITIVE THOUGHTS, POSITIVE VIBES!

365

APRIL 4TH

Most people who know me know the elephant is my favorite animal. Known for its remarkable memory, the elephant embodies simplicity and contentment, thriving on just the essentials for a happy and free life. This incredible animal teaches us valuable lessons about finding joy in simplicity. It's not always about the big house on the hill, the fancy cars, or a truckload of money. True happiness often comes from embracing life's simple pleasures and discovering what genuinely brings us joy. The elephant reminds us that happiness comes in many forms and fashions—it's all about finding what works for us and living with purpose and ease.

365

APRIL 5TH

Because of grace, I stand here today! What is grace? Grace gets me through my struggles. Grace allows me to be me. You accepted this imperfect person and say it's ok. It's ok to be you, because God has got your back.

Grace allows us to give the world the best we have to offer and fine tune those things we need to. God loves us for who we are and he wants you to stand tall and love who you are today. Today is your day to love you!

POSITIVE THOUGHTS, POSITIVE VIBES!

365

APRIL 6ᵀᴴ

I'm telling you to never give up on you. Don't throw in the towel. It's tough, you turn to the left and right and nothing is working out. Your friends are few and far between. It's ok, because this is life.

You are being tested and it's time to look within, my friend. Like the song says, "trouble don't last always," and today is your day. You are still standing because something about you doesn't quit.

Look for and think of something positive and start with that. Your view point and perspective can provide what you need to keep moving forward.

365

APRIL 7ᵀᴴ

It's time to put who you were behind you and find out who you are. Most of us spend our lives not truly knowing who we are.

You take care of this and that, please others and become Mr. or Ms. Dependable. The you gets lost in the sauce.

It's time to stir things up and look within to see the true you. Your light is ready to shine if you can open the blinds. The world needs to have the real you so that the ones who need your blessing will receive it.

We all have something to offer and let's make it as pure and true as possible.

365

APRIL 8TH

I wasn't sure how I would get through it. I wasn't sure how I was going to get past it, and it took some time for me to break free. It was time for me to breathe again. It's so important that we continue to balance ourselves to make sure we're surrounded by people who will energize our mind, body, and soul.

I thought I had reached the end of the road until my angel appeared. That's right. If we keep our eyes open, that person will appear to lift our spirits and make themselves available.

APRIL 9TH

BE FREE. FEEL FREE.

It's no fun waking up every morning thinking about fifty million problems to solve. Or carrying around burdens and guilt about something you said or did.

You are the only one who can free yourself from it all. Allow at least a few moments a day to feel free.

Some problems you will have to let go of and understand that we don't always say or do the right things. You give the world YOU; the best you have to offer. That has to be good enough!

365

APRIL 10TH

Wake up and decide to be you. That's right, I'm going to offer the world the real deal. I'm not going to sit and wonder if people will like it or not.

Is what I have to offer worthy enough? I need to make everyone happy with what they see on the outside. Your mindset may be in the wrong place. It's on the outside and you already forgot about the inside. That's where the real you is! Let that light shine baby and attract the ones who deserve it. If it works for them that's cool, if not, keep on keeping on!

365

APRIL 11TH

I thought I was living my best life… car, house, marriage you name it. I was moving too fast. I didn't take a step back to realize that I need to find myself. That's right, who the heck am I?

Make sure to take care of yourself, find out who you are so you don't lose yourself in the midst of trying to live your best life. It all starts from within, going deep down and letting the true 'you' come out. How cool is it, when you're able to find out who you are and what your purpose, passion and reason for living is? Yes, car, house and marriage can enhance your happiness but finding the true 'you' is priceless.

365

APRIL 12ᵀᴴ

Relationships are so important to our everyday well-being. Family, friends, lovers they all hold different energies to keep us balanced. Keeping the communication lines open with honesty will lead to understanding. Through understanding comes respect and with respect comes presence.

The ability to be who you are allows for the relationships to grow positively. It's all about the people and energy that surrounds you, which allows your spirit to feel free.

Enjoy those wonderful relationships and accept them in whatever form they hold. Be present!

APRIL 13TH

Circumstances can change your life in the blink of an eye. Don't let adversity steer your spirit into a different direction.

This storm shall pass and another one will come. It's up to you to see the big picture and figure out how to handle the situation when it arises. You can create change by looking at your circumstances from a different perspective.

See the good first and let that be your driving force. Surround yourself with people who inspire your spirit and offer help in your time of need. From within, you have the power to shine no matter what you are going through.

365

APRIL 14ᵀᴴ

You have a plan and God has a plan. Which one is best? You woke up this morning moving forward with your plan. Things rolling right along until that bump in the road that throws things off the path. You're not sure which way to turn and what the next move should be. That's when you ask God for help. You ask for help with your current plan but He has another.

Having faith will allow you to detour into God's plan for you. It allows Him to order your steps and lead the way. It will smooth things out in time. Be still and let the winds from up above put your spirit on the right path.

365

APRIL 15ᵀᴴ

You know that "No parking on the dance floor" by Midnight Star, is one of my favorite songs. It just moves through your body in a way and that booty start to shake.

Just like in life, you need to keep those juices flowing, energize your mind, body, and soul and get to groovin'. The hook will have you shaking yourself in the right direction, putting you around the right people and allowing you to get your mojo back. Like the song says, "it's so easy to rock baby" you are the DJ in control of the right mix that will keep you moving on the dance floor.

365

APRIL 16TH

There's a saying, "Take some time to smell the roses." It means, take a moment and enjoy the beauty that is all around you.

This is a great way to start creating positivity in your life. Take a moment to enjoy the flowers, birds, the sunset, and a full moon. Don't run around all day and ignore what is simply beautiful around you. Beauty represents good, and the good was created by God.

Open your eyes to His creations and enjoy your ability to take it in.

365

APRIL 17TH

Have you spent most of your life giving it away? Hoping instead of living? Your best life is in the present.

Find joy in the little things, embrace those dreams and revelations that allow you to live in the now. Your living starts today. The past is behind you, and none of us have the power to predict the future.

Living your best life starts from within. Opening your heart for peace, a peace that only you can find. Go get your peace and start livin' my friend, no more existing!

APRIL 18ᵀᴴ

Every year there is a National Acts of Kindness Day. We did an amazing social media push encouraging everyone to discuss different ways to be kinder to each other. Remember acts of the kindness is a part of our everyday living.

Show love, share a hug, send a card, check in on a neighbor. Take a moment to think of others, pay it forward and encourage someone else to do the same. Allow your light to shine to positively impact others, spread that sunshine and help move those clouds out of the way. Be true in the love you share and allow the rippling effect to create the change you want to see.

365

APRIL 19TH

Today was the best day, do you know why? Because I took some time to focus on me. I called off of work, went back home and jumped right into bed, LOL.

Minimize the noise of the world and dive in for some peace. A little "me time" is so important to keep yourself balanced for the things ahead. I know the list is long, and so many things to do but don't forget the "me time." Once you have rested in bed for a little, head over to that happy place, grab some dinner or drink or just spend some time doing nothing. Today was the best day because I took a little time out for me.

APRIL 20ᵀᴴ

We meet people for a reason. They can become a blessing or a lesson on our journey. Taking the time to understand one another is a form of LOVE. Our differences become less obvious and the unknown more common.

There is an old saying, "Love thy neighbor," and we are all neighbors looking for the same thing in life. There is an opportunity to show love and be loved.

Share a little love today. Offer a smile, a kind word or a helping hand. Fill your soul with positive energy and you will experience the power of LOVE.

APRIL 21ˢᵀ

Sometimes it's worth talking to a stranger. You don't know the person in line at the store, the person on the bus, or at the football game. But the person next to you can offer a refreshing spirit that can brighten up your day.

It's simple. No judgement, no objective, no need. Just connection. An opportunity to strike up a conversation about anything can lead to a moment. That's a moment for you to be you and share the positivity you have to offer. Enjoy the moment and let time be still within the conversation of a stranger.

365

APRIL 22ND

Are you ready to plant your garden?

First thing is to clear out all the weeds. Just like in our lives, we must weed out the ugly in order to plant something new.

Cultivate the soil, cleanse your soul and put the past behind you. Plant those seeds and water daily. Put yourself around motivational people and read your daily devotional to feed your soul.

TAKE THE NECESSARY STEPS AND WATCH YOUR GROWTH.

365

APRIL 23RD

I woke up this morning and realized that God has a greater plan for me. I believe in me. I honor who I am and I continue my growth to see all of the gifts that He has bestowed upon me. These gifts I continue to share with the world. I embrace the power that they behold. Forever thankful, forever appreciative of all of the things that I have around me, which is giving me the opportunity to give. What are my gifts? What do I have to offer to the world? Start with just being you! Think about the things you are passionate about and run with that. You will have the ability to give, to grow and to impact so many people... it will be the best feeling ever.

365

APRIL 24TH

You gotta do it your way! Today you're not listening to anyone else's suggestions or ideas. You've got all the answers and when things go wrong it's someone else's fault. Well, it looks like you need a new outlook. Don't wait until the "stuff" hits the fan before you understand it's time to open up.

Allow others to assist, offer opinions and add a little something. Get that pot mixing with tons of variety. Your way or the highway might not work this time.

Let's open up and add a little something different. You might be pleasantly surprised.

365

APRIL 25TH

It's not about the destination, but the road traveled. It's not about where you are going but how you get there. That includes all of the pit stops and fill-ups along the way. These things help shape and prepare you for what is waiting.

Things always have a way of working themselves out. The pot holes, road closures and detours are a part of the journey. Continue to move forward and stay focused. You will be surprised where the road leads you.

365

APRIL 26TH

You woke up this morning and finally realized you have been giving the world second best. What happened to the best you have to offer or the best of you?

Are you lost in the sauce, swimming around wondering where you went? The good part is you can start today finding you, the true and real you.

Start pleasing you first and the awesome light you have will shine bright. It's time to start blessing the world with the best you.

POSITIVE THOUGHTS, POSITIVE VIBES!

365

APRIL 27TH

A simple encounter can lead to friendship for life. You had no idea that the person you just met would have your back for life. Why do we connect with some and not others? What makes a connection special or above the rest?

We see similarities in people that draw us in. It could be a spiritual, work, or other connection. There are many different reasons why we connect. The spirit of that person could be easy like Sunday morning. If the connection is real, then just looking within will provide the answer. We met for a reason and our connection has purpose. Enjoy the simplicity of it.

365

APRIL 28TH

We use the words, "I'm sorry" often enough. Apologies can sometimes be short lived if the actions don't follow.

They say if a person doesn't change their behavior, then why apologize?

Are we using the word sorry to make ourselves feel ok about our actions? Or are we really honest about changing our behavior to match the words we say and use. I guess time will tell if the words match the action.

THEY SAY YOUR WORD IS YOUR BOND. SO HOLD TRUE TO YOU.

365

APRIL 29TH

There will be times in our lives when the word *reassurance* will appear. Our vulnerability will provide an opportunity for someone or something to make you feel safe, less afraid, upset or have doubt.

When someone provides that reassurance, that who you are and what you have to offer is just right, your comfort level will grow and your doubt will fade. This reassurance will give you the chance to be the true you. That's right the true you is what the world needs.

365

APRIL 30ᵀᴴ

I'm not tired yet. They sang that song in church growing up -- hand clapping, foot stomping, singing and smiling. Nothing but joy and positive energy flowing throughout the building. You've been knocked around, can't find your way, or not sure who to call when you need a friend. You're not tired yet because you have been through the struggle before. I can see you still standing trying to get stronger day by day. Today you look within for the strength to get through this as well. Come on, get up, start that hand clapping, foot stomping, do a dance and sing that song! I can see your glow shining through. You're not tired yet because God just gave you a new dance.

365

MAY 1ST

In the movie Lion Guard Bunga sang "Zuka Zama". It's a funny little song with lots of meaning. In Swahili it means, "Pop up, dive in."

Today may be your day to pop up and dive in. Dive in and let your heart sing and your soul feel. Open up and breathe new air and new life in the old life you have been living. Love the new life that's in right in front of you. Sing that song, dance that dance. Zuka Zuma might just be the song you need to wake up and dive in.

365

MAY 2ND

I feel so blessed. I have the best kids, and the perfect neighbors in the perfect neighborhood. I'm grateful to have all of the basic things that sometimes, we take for granted. It's so important for us, every morning, to thank God for all that we have.

Through my nonprofit Foundation I see the struggles many families are going through.

As we continue to move forward, take note that it all starts now, in the present. Create that solid foundation now that will create the balance you need in the future.

www.pmjfoundation.org

365

MAY 3RD

I miss my daddy.... when we lose a loved one, they will always be missed. But like they say, he is always with me. I know why, 'cause there goes the feather. That feather my dad kept in his truck and every once in a while, that feather will pop up. I can be leaving the grocery store, mowing the lawn or sitting in my backyard. At the right moment and time, that feather will pop up. That loved one will send you a sign, letting you know it's ok. It's ok to move on and keep living. Pay attention to the little signs they leave; the beauty of their spirit will always be with you.

365

MAY 4TH

They thought they had you down for the count. You know the ones that call you to see if you're doing not so well. We have folks around us that look for the bad and forget about the good.

Well, it's time, my friends, to change that inner circle. Surround yourself with people who lift your spirit, rejuvenate your soul and stimulate your mind.

It's a new day with a new outlook on life. It's all because you made changes to your environment in a positive way.

365

MAY 5<u>TH</u>

Man, I am on a roll today. Everything is going just fine. Everything is working out. I have had some great conversations with some amazing people. All of my things are getting done. Today is what I'm calling an amazing day.

Sometimes we need to take some time and recognize those awesome days when they happen. Yeah, I know, not every day is going to feel like today, but today I recognize it as being an awesome day. We can take those positive juices to help propel us through those tough times. So, you know what my friends? I am gonna soak up this awesome day and spread a little sunshine with it.

365

MAY 6TH

James Brown said it best "I feel good." You know what? I feel so good I started dancing and singing in the living room. Don't go laughing at me, I do that often LOL. That's how good I felt.

I'm not sure of the source but it really doesn't matter sometimes. Soak up the good and let those good vibes flow. Dance, sing and laugh your way into allowing your spirit to get the juice it needs. Get those feet moving and feel-good baby.

365

MAY 7TH

Many of you know the story by now. My father passed away in 2015 from a massive heart attack. Some might say, as a form of therapy, I started writing and posting Positive messages on social media. My friend and publisher, Kathleen J. Shields said you need to write a book. So ever since, I've been writing these short daily affirmations for everyone.

We all have something to share, a talent or gift. Feel free to share this message along with any of the daily affirmations I write. Together we will sprinkle a little more Positive Vibes into the world.

MAY 8TH

LOOK HOW BEAUTIFUL YOU ARE.

Today is the day you decided to accept the person that you see in the mirror. Your smile, eyes, hair it all belongs to you.

EMBRACE THE PERSON
THAT GOD MADE.

You look pretty darn good to me. Your beauty lies within; your soul shines because you appreciate the progress that's been made.

365

MAY 9TH

Saying, "I love you," can come in many different forms. Sometimes we don't say it or show it enough. We all get caught up in the rat race of life. There is always too much to do with too little time.

Appreciating the people in your circle can sometimes take a back seat.

Find a way to show your love so even when you don't say it people feel it. Live a life filled with it so, "I Love You," will shine brightly from your spirit.

When a person can feel it, that love… that means way more than saying it.

365

MAY 10TH

The connection between two people can add positivity to one's life. One can define intimacy as, any action that enhances the mind/heart connection between two people. Even just sitting quietly holding hands is intimate with the right person.

Connection is important. It allows the mind, body and soul to grow and evolve. Be willing to feel the intimacy one has to offer and enjoy the beauty it holds.

POSITIVE THOUGHTS, POSITIVE VIBES!

365

MAY 11TH

Pillow talk. What is pillow talk? They say it's an opportunity where you can sit down with someone and just completely open up. Having that safe space where you can talk about anything and everything.

We all wish and hope for that someone that we can talk with. To lay our heads on a pillow, relax and have the opportunity to completely be ourselves. That's what it's all about, the opportunity to completely be yourself, and be in that safe space, to let someone else know what you're thinking, feeling or what you desire.

365

MAY 12TH

One of the greatest gifts someone can give is their soul. It means they completely trust you, and feel comfortable with who you are and where you are.

The ability to be vulnerable from within, and allowing your feelings to be shared can be terrifying. It means sharing your deepest thoughts, wants, desires. The effects of life experiences have shaped you. You are a different person today than you were yesterday.

Hopefully you will be blessed with that opportunity to be freed, in order to be free.

365

MAY 13TH

We will meet many people in our lifetime but who is truly there for you? How will you know? When times are tough or going well who can you turn to when all heck breaks loose? Can they lift your spirits and help you through it?

We all will need someone to be there when we need them most. An angel will be waiting in the wings. The key is to be open minded when they show up. It could be the one you least expect and the beauty in that is priceless.

SO, WHO IS TRULY IN YOUR CORNER?

365

MAY 14TH

One of the greatest gifts my mother gave me was an introduction to God. There is importance in having a relationship with the creator of the universe. That relationship has taken on many forms over the years.

When I discuss having a relationship with God amongst others, I relay that it's your own personal relationship. It belongs to you. It's not what others want it to be. It is yours and yours alone. Whether it's a happy time or a time of need, God comes to you in the way He chooses. Hold strong to this and let the light God has for you shine through.

365

MAY 15TH

Just when one thing goes right another thing goes wrong. You just can't get ahead it seems, and the light at the end of the tunnel looks dim. How can you breathe when it never stops?

DID YOU ASK GOD FOR HELP?

You can talk to Him and He will hear you. He might send you an angel. Allow your mind to rest for a bit and give you the strength to get through it. Asking God for help allows your mind to pause and focus on Him. This might be the little thing you need to reevaluate and increase your faith.

365

MAY 16TH

NATIONAL DO SOMETHING GOOD FOR YOUR NEIGHBOR DAY

Do you know your neighbors? Today may be a good day to meet them. Today is the perfect reminder that the simple act of kindness can make a world of difference. Whether it's offering a helping hand, sharing a smile, or just checking in to see how someone's doing, small gestures of care create a ripple effect of warmth and community. We're all in this together, and sometimes, it's the people right next door who need us most. So, let's make today a celebration of connection.

365

MAY 17ᵀᴴ

Today I will make sure to appreciate everything that I have and I am. Yesterday was a crazy day filled with drama, uncertainty, stress but also some joys. Let's focus on those joys and allow that to start our day.

Today you will make sure to take a few minutes to be thankful for what you have and who you are. Start with some positivity and allow that to help you with the other stuff.

365

MAY 18TH

You may ask yourself how you can communicate better and have a truly good conversation? Well communicating is easy, right? You just talk, say what's on your mind and people will understand. Not so fast there, it takes more than that. We must be able to listen, feel and articulate what's on our mind.

Trying to interpret what someone is trying to say isn't always easy. We all have different ways of communicating and the willingness to understand each other is key. Taking the time to listen and talking through it can provide a positive outcome in the situation.

365

MAY 19TH

In this crazy world we live in, sometimes we forget that love conquers hate and unity eliminates division. We must be open to building bridges, instead of perpetuating hate, anger and ignorance.

Through love comes understanding and the ability to see past ourselves. We cannot let our egos cloud a pathway of being open-minded.

You control what you feel for others. Can you see their beauty or just their faults? Can you see beyond what might hurt and see what can heal?

Start with positivity and see what you get!

365

MAY 20TH

There is a huge difference between helping others and enabling others. We have to take a step back to see if the help we are offering is beneficial. Someone might just need to feel a little fire to get going.

Holding folks accountable for their actions is not always a bad thing. Make sure the help you are offering will allow that person to be their own person.

Don't allow them to feed off your spirit. This is a draining process. Life is about balance. We need to keep ourselves well balanced in order to see the difference.

MAY 21ST

There are such a thing as angels. In your time of need someone or something will appear. Not sure what form or shape but yes, an angel. A form of love will appear that will comfort the soul and rejuvenate the spirit. Are you ready?

Sometimes we're not ready to take in what the angel has to offer. The vulnerability of a person might just allow them to see and feel the security that angel offers. We all need a helping hand, someone or something that will be there for us at the right time.

THE BEAUTY IS IN RECOGNIZING IT
AND APPRECIATING IT.

365

MAY 22<u>ND</u>

Are you wondering why the things you used to do are not happening anymore?

How is your spirit? Are you broken? The world has worn you out and you can't find your juice. Is it possible to break away from the rat race for a little? Can you clear your thoughts to get back to you?

In order to offer the best you, you must get back to you. The things that gave you peace need to find a place in your heart again. Piece by piece today is your day to do and be you.

MAY 23<u>RD</u>

You get up every morning and you give it your all. Consider giving it 100% or close to it. Yet, you discover that is not enough or people still need more.

Are you putting your energy in the wrong people or places? Do you feel drained or inspired to give more? Take a step back and analyze the steps you are taking.

Make sure balance is a part of your daily vocabulary. Without balance you will feel drained. Don't allow too much taking without giving.

Take some time out to energize yourself. Give but be cautious in where and to whom you might be giving to.

365

MAY 24TH

You will face moments that test your strength and willpower. These challenges can make you a stronger person and allow you to learn some valuable lessons.

Our growth comes through challenges and our ability to move forward. That's what makes us who we are. Look for the silver lining and allow a little light in to help get you through.

It's not always an easy ride, but you do have the ability to get through it.

365

MAY 25TH

I love the song by Lakeside, "There's something about that woman."

You know the one, that special someone that you think about often. You're pretty fond of the way they talk, walk and make you feel. Allow yourself to be open, free and absorb the positive vibes.

If you ever had a real love, then you know there's something about that person that makes your heart sing. Beholding the beauty of allowing yourself to feel, gives the opportunity to appreciate the true love.

365

MAY 26TH

They say your beauty is in your openness. Yes, you are real and offer yourself in a way to be appreciated and accepted. You can be straight forward and kind at the same time.

The beauty of all of this, is giving the world a chance to feel the real you. Openness can be a very powerful thing, allowing others in to accept what you have to offer. Through this you allow, attract and distract the ones who enter your orbit.

Embrace the power and enjoy the beauty of being you. It has a place within the right space.

MAY 27TH

Attraction starts from within.

Physical attraction is common but mental attraction can be hard to find. That person that makes your heart sing and your spirit soar. How does your spirit feel when you speak or are in the presence of that person?

Do they energize your mind, body and soul in ways that the physical cannot?

Yes, we all enjoy a physical attraction but without the mental, the physical will fade. Surround yourself with people that simulate your mind which in turn will fuel your spirit.

365

MAY 28TH

A song in my rotation includes the phrase, "you fight on." Trouble doesn't always last, but I hear you. You have been knocked down, felt alone, stumbled a few times but yes, "you fight on." You fight on because today and every day you continue to work towards being and giving your best.

Sing that song that lifts your spirit, wear that smile and let your light shine. You have been through tough times before, so today and every day, allow the positive in and it will help you fight on.

365

MAY 29TH

They say always give 100%, well today maybe 75% is all you have. Let that be enough for today and use the other 25% as fuel for tomorrow.

"There's never enough time." Well, enough time for what? Sometimes good enough is good enough.

Don't continue to push yourself to the limit with no room to breathe. Remember giving your all is not always easy. You give your best day in and day out and today you did the same.

RECHARGE UP AND REFUEL!

365

MAY 30TH

If we've learned anything, we know that people need people! It's time to go out there and get your groove back, offer up a hug, smile, a kind word. During these past few years, we all needed each other to get through some tough times. Now we could all use some cheering....

The power of physical connection is so important to the mind, body and soul. Yes, we figured it out, how to get by without it, but it sure feels good to get back to those old times of connection.

365

MAY 31ST

NATIONAL SMILE DAY

It's a known fact that a smile releases endorphins, which improve your mood, help you relax, and lowers your blood pressure. Smiling is good for your health and so is positive thinking.

So today, along with every day, but especially today, smile! Smile with your mouth, smile with your eyes, smile with your heart. The brighter your smile, the more good it will do for yourself as well as others. Don't be shy. Just smile.

365

JUNE 1ST

NATIONAL SAY SOMETHING NICE DAY

Today, let's use the power of words to lift each other up and spread positivity. A kind compliment, a thoughtful word, or a genuine expression of gratitude can brighten someone's day and remind them of their worth.

Remember, kindness is contagious. When you speak with compassion, you create a ripple effect that can inspire others to do the same.

POSITIVE THOUGHTS, POSITIVE VIBES!

365

JUNE 2ᴺᴰ

I think Al Jarreau said it best, "You can be what you want to. All you need is to get your boogie down." Sounds like you might need a few new moves or a change of pace. Getting stuck in your comfort or safe zone might not be what's best. I get it -- change is scary, darn right frightening sometimes, but you want peace, happiness and to feel free. Put a plan together, start with small steps which might lead to a pretty good groove. We can't wait to see what your 'boogie down' looks like. The world is waiting for the best you that you have to offer and getting out of your comfort zone might be the answer.

JUNE 3RD

WHO DO YOU LOOK UP TO?

A role model, person you admire or one who inspires you? We are surrounded by all types of people. You can choose whom you would like to be in your circle or orbit.

Make sure the one you look up to is feeding you the positivity that you need. Feed off of the ones who inspire you and allow that to fuel your fire from within.

Our spirit needs to feed off of good energy and yes that can come from many sources including the ones you look up too.

365

JUNE 4TH

Today is the day you make the first step. God promised if you make the first step, He will make the second. You are making strides to add a little more positivity in your life. Join the positive vibes movement and continue to do the things you need to do to live the life you want.

Create that vibe tribe of genuine people and allow them to support and inspire you moving forward. Step one today, will lead to many more steps moving forward. Continue making strides and allow your passion for living your best life to shine.

365

JUNE 5TH

I thought we were friends? You told me I was your best friend, the one you could turn to in your time of need. But it feels like the friendship has fizzled. You have turned cold and distant. I continue to reach out and offer comfort but you turn me away. Why?

What happened to understanding that true friendship means opening up when things get tough? Now is not the time to push me away, instead, bring me in close. I'm here for you. Know that my friendship is true.

I GOT YOUR BACK!

365

JUNE 6ᵀᴴ

How beautiful is it when someone truly loves you? I mean, truly loves the person from within. Not a fantasy, dream or someone from your favorite romance novel. The feeling when someone is in "Awe" of you! Revered, admired, adored, appreciated, cherished, the list goes on.

Your ability to feel safe in their presence, completely comfortable in being who you are and what you offer, is a gift. No judgement, a safe space of vulnerability that will allow your love to grow.

365

JUNE 7TH

Mary Mary said it best, "take the shackles off my feet so I can dance."

Free yourself from the negative energy of the world. The people in your circle could be holding you back from your blessing. Those feet of yours would love to shuffle or even do the twist but Chubby Checker can't help you with this one.

Take the next step, identify the people and things that are holding you back. Make the change towards positive living. It will not be easy but it will be necessary in order for you to step out onto the dance floor ahead.

JUNE 8TH

Are you in search for that something that makes your spirit feel good? It can come in all form's shapes, and sizes, through people, things, and of course what you are passionate about. It's very important to put yourself around positive energy and positive people. It feels like a fresh cool breeze or a fresh cup of orange juice.

Never stop searching for something that makes your spirit feel good, this is what helps create the balance in our lives. The ability to create balance is so important. So, continue to search for the things that make you feel good.

365

JUNE 9TH

Scared to let people get to know you? Some people might be shy, bashful or introverted. Maybe the issue is every time you give you get hurt. People don't know how to appreciate who you are. So, they try to change you, put you down and put a dimmer on your light.

Well dimming the light won't work today because God made you in his image. Greatness is all over you and you must continue to share yourself. Someone out there needs your spirit. They need to see your smile. Because today your smile looks brighter than ever.

365

JUNE 10TH

RAISE SOMEONE UP, PLEASE!

We spend so much time focusing on our own needs that we need to help someone else, too. It doesn't take much; a listening ear, a kind word or just spending a little time. Reach out and offer a helping hand to a friend in need.

Ask someone how they are truly feeling and listen without judgment or opinion. It feels great making someone else feel good and it will give your spirit a positive boost!

365

JUNE 11TH

It's time to jump! That's right, time to jump. What are you waiting for, the perfect moment, time or place? The stars may never align unless you jump. Yes, you might disappoint a few folks, be judged, or even be laughed at. But now is the best time. You will never know what lies ahead if you don't.

Something better is waiting on the other side. Go start that business, write that book, fall in love and even fly across the world. Today is your day to jump into the future with a whole new outlook.

365

JUNE 12ᵀᴴ

We have all been through the fire and prayed for rain. What is your testimony? Where have you come from to take you to the place you must go? Do you even know where you would like to be? What does the present look like and how will it lead you into the future?

They say trouble doesn't last and we all have a story to share. Share your testimony so that it might help someone else get through their storm. Wash away some of those troubles with a little inspiration.

365

JUNE 13ᵀᴴ

Let's talk about enlightenment. Your spiritual growth allows for a deeper awareness of you who are. We would all love to know our purpose in life, who we are and what we have to offer. Finding peace or acceptance from within can allow for this transformation to occur. It will only happen when as they say "the time is right." A major life change could be the cause for the awakening to start (death in the family, change in family dynamics, health issues). Once you start to comprehend that something is happening within, allow it to take form.

Continue to let the positivity in and drive the negativity out.

365

JUNE 14TH

Do we really know who we are? The person that people see, is that really the true you or a facade? It's not always easy to give the world the true you.

Our true selves are forever evolving because we are always in growth mode. Through growth, we understand ourselves better; feeling more and more comfortable in our own skin.

JUST LOVE YOURSELF!

Love what you know about yourself and share that with the world. The ones who truly appreciate it will see the beauty in you!

JUNE 15ᵀᴴ

I was driving down the street and Jonathan McReynolds said, "I will make room for you." Today is the day when you can move it over. You have to allow space for the good to come in.

Negativity will take over and not allow your mind, body and soul to be still. In order to see and feel your blessings, you need some still time.

Push aside as much as you can and let the good that is there shine through. Make the first step and God will help with the next one.

365

JUNE 16TH

I know you see the smile on my face. My two boys bring me so much joy. When God blesses you with such perfection, all you can do is smile. We laugh, we cry, we talk and we walk.

We keep our eyes on the future with nothing but positive thoughts flowing. I give them my best and they do the same.

I'm just gonna keep on smiling, because smiling makes me feel good and it shows. I'm living my best life because of my boys.

365

JUNE 17<u>TH</u>

The Lord said it, 'and bless it be to rock and let the God of my salvation be exalted'. Today is the day that you claim it.

You claim the victory, happiness, and your peace. Look upon the Lord because the victory is yours. That new job, new book you're going to write and that new relationship right around the corner.

Enjoy the positive energy flowing because you gave Him the praise first "when the praises go up, the blessing come down."

365

JUNE 18TH

It's not always easy to see the light at the end of the tunnel. People often say things will get better, that tough times don't last forever, and you'll get through it. But you've faced challenge after challenge, and it feels difficult just to make your way through the tunnel.

Here's what you need to remember: you've always had the strength to keep moving forward. Take a moment to pause, reflect on your surroundings, and make small changes where you can. Keep moving forward, step by step, and you'll start to see that little glimmer of hope waiting for you at the end of the tunnel.

365

JUNE 19TH

The loss of a loved one changes us. In some ways we can't always explain. Hurt, pain, sorrow and anger can consume us during that time. To ease the emotions people tell us to think about the good times.

How do we deal with it all? How do we allow our soul to grieve in peace? Remember that the spirit lives on. Why not have a chat with that loved one. I talk to my daddy every day. I ask him to guide my steps. Some might say that's silly for a 46-year-old, but it gives me peace.

Peace in the midst of the journey is just what might be needed.

JUNE 20TH

Healing comes in time and allowing you that time is so important. We're all different and the healing process is yours and yours only. The loss of a loved one, family transition, job loss or just trying to find your way, is hard.

You must take time to allow your mind, body and soul to heal. The good part is, while doing the healing process, reflection can occur. This gives you a chance to tap into the strength and courage you never knew you had. A different you is already in the making. Embrace the transformation that healing can do.

365

JUNE 21ST

My youngest son, Harrison, loves being outside, whether he's catching bugs or looking for slugs late at night, being outdoors makes him happy.

God's little creatures can offer a sense of gratification. Whether it's riding scooters, or swinging on a swing, take a few minutes to enjoy the peacefulness of the outdoors. It's simplistic, no drama, no over thinking.

Nature allows you to just be and enjoy what life has to offer. You might be surprised how good it makes your spirit feel.

365

JUNE 22ᴺᴰ

I found my path or at least the road I should travel. Man, I have lost a lot, cried a few tears and was unsure on a number of occasions. But today it feels good to know I'm where I need to be.

My mind, body and soul are in the right place and space. The feeling was uncomfortable, but I found my way through it. God has a pathway, road, or journey just for you.

Believe in it and keep moving forward on your path because the only person stopping you from this, is you.

JUNE 23RD

Does death change us? When a loved one leaves this earth does it have a positive or negative effect on you? Of course, we would love to have that person for another day but yesterday was that day.

We have a chance now to remember the good times and think about the things learned. That's right, we learn more about ourselves through death. Our perception and perspective changes, positive or negative, is up to you!

365

JUNE 24ᵀᴴ

Why are so many people unhappy? What would make you happy? Love, money, less work and more vacation time? The stress of everyday living can weigh on the mind, body and soul. It can have you spinning in all different directions and keep you from your happiness.

They say, "Beauty is in the eye of the beholder." Well, happiness is too. You hold the key to your door of happiness. Look for the few simple things that make you happy and focus on them. You will be surprised how light your spirit will get and how peaceful you may feel.

365

JUNE 25TH

It's time to do something different. Get out of that rut and start thinking outside of the box. You sit and wish things would change but do nothing about it! Can you see it or maybe feel something new happening? Well, time has come to step out on faith and do it. I get it, still trying to figure out what you will be when you grow up. Well, start doing and you might be surprised. The outcome could be pretty positive. At the end of the day give it your best and make that initial step. Keep moving forward and don't be afraid of the detours, road block or potholes. You're likely to end up on the right path.

JUNE 26TH

Where can you find happiness? We all want to be happy, right? What does happiness look or feel like? It includes positive thinking, pleasant emotions, and some form of satisfaction. Start with appreciation for the good in your life.

Count your many blessings, some are as simple as waking up in the morning. Create that list of the things you want to accomplish. You are in charge of what your happiness looks and feels like.

Just be and soak in all the good around you. Remember that your happiness comes from within.

365

JUNE 27TH

You know what? I'm stepping it up today. Going the extra mile, thinking outside the box, being the me I want to be.

Don't let the day-to-day tasks of the world bring you down. Slap reality right in the face and put one foot in front of the other. Push a few things aside and get back to being you.

You can only do what you can do! By taking care of yourself you will have the ability to take care of others. Focus on you a little today and allow your positivity to shine through.

365

JUNE 28TH

I'm sitting here and you know I have it figured out. Go left, go right, go any which way. Life can have you twisting and turning in all different directions. You second guess your moves, ask for suggestions and it's just not feeling right.

Take the leap! What do you have to lose? Ok it might not work out the way you planned it but it might work out for the best. Yes, I wrote that book, I cleaned up my resume, I changed careers. Really guys, who has it all figured out? Today… just go with it and start living. I bet something is gonna work out and I'm thinking the change will be good.

365

JUNE 29TH

It's so important to take the time out to say thank you. You are never too busy to say thank you. Always take the time out to tell someone you appreciate them for who they are, and everything that they've done for you.

Thank you might not seem like much, but just the ability to say thank you to someone, just to show that you appreciate everything that they do for you is so important. People want to feel appreciated. By saying thank you or offering a kind word, that's how you do it.

THANK YOU FOR JUST BEING YOU!

365

JUNE 30TH

We all have control of the type of life we want to live. Most of us would love to live a happy life filled with positivity. Of course, there will be some bumps in the road, but our choices decide that.

Also, things that you have no control of will try to consume you. Allow how you would like to live to lead the way.

Take a few minutes every morning to balance yourself with positive thoughts that will keep you on the right path. Remember you have the power to live the best life you want.

365

JULY 1ST

You hear people talking about a happy place. What is that? An actual place you travel to for some peace and quiet? Could it be the beach, church, wooded area, etc. or is it something that you do? Being in a happy place or space is essential to creating balance in your life. Getting away from the hustle and bustle of the world allows you to feel peace. We all deserve that! It will allow us to give our best to the world. A happier you!

POSITIVE THOUGHTS, POSITIVE VIBES!

JULY 2<u>ND</u>

Are we truly connected? In a society where technology has taken over, the word "conversation" takes on a different meaning. Texting and email is how we communicate now. What happened to the old-fashioned face-to-face conversation and taking a few minutes to call someone and chat? A text can be misinterpreted and lacks emotion. As humans, we carry emotions and that's how we express ourselves. Through speaking and body language we can best interpret what someone is saying. Whether positive or negative the best interpretation is what we all need. Let's talk.

365

JULY 3RD

What is really important to You?

What are the things that really matter in life? A good job, big house, fancy car? I think what happens is we let "stuff" get in the way. Things seem to be what we feel are important. You keep working towards things that will leave you empty in the end. Maybe today you just need a nice hug, a little breathing room, or an ear to listen. Peace or at least feeling peace might be the most important. Because when we feel peaceful, we see the world differently. It gives us the ability to really feel what is important. Simple pleasures are not so hard to come by.

365

JULY 4TH

My mother sang a song in church, "Victory is Mine." What would you consider your victory? Are you on the right path and have the right mind set to enjoy your victory?

Remember it's all yours! How you feel, think, love and live, belongs to you. Your victory is waiting for you to enjoy and it will unfold itself when your soul is ready.

Don't go looking for it because it might pass you by. Be still and allow the positive energy all around you to lead you in the right direction.

JULY 5TH

When I look at my two sons, I marvel in their simplicity. Most of us adults don't get it, in the way they do.

Our needs and wants are different. They want love, food, shelter, maybe a few pieces of candy and a toy or two. Feeling safe is most important.

We should all take a moment to bask in the pure simplicity of living in the way they do. Life might not be as difficult if we keep it simple. Take what they give us from within and allow our growth to form from that.

365

JULY 6TH

They say time rules us all, and it often feels like there's never enough of it. The world moves so fast that finding a moment to breathe can seem nearly impossible.

We get caught up in the endless tasks, focusing on everything that needs fixing, and sometimes overlooking the good things happening around us.

Our perception of time can shape how we use it. Take a step back, prioritize what truly matters each day, and always make room to breathe.

365

JULY 7TH

Stop giving away your peace. You all know it's very difficult to find peace or what might be considered your peace. Once you do, you must own it, protect and create those boundaries.

Yes, we all need help, support and to give, but protecting your peace through the process is essential. Some might not understand it but your ability to give back comes from the peace you have within.

POSITIVE THOUGHTS, POSITIVE VIBES!

365

JULY 8TH

Try this. Stand at a playground and watch the children play. The simplicity of it is beautiful. It doesn't matter the shade, height or even if they speak the same language - they play.

Play is an awesome way to communicate. It allows the spirit to be free. The goal is simple: have fun. When we look into the eyes of a child, the innocence in them is what life is all about.

Try not complicating what life has to offer. Focus on all of the positivity around you.

365

JULY 9TH

People might ask,
"Why do you do the things you do?"

Well, I'm just being me. That's right, being you is a cool thing. You know that the ones who want to get it, will get it!

There is no need to compromise your core self to fit in. We all have different qualities about us, so let yours shine. Through that you will attract the right ones and detract the ones not needed in your mix.

I'm looking forward to seeing the real you, if you like it, then that's good enough.

JULY 10TH

You hear it time and time again in church. Don't let anyone steal your joy. Well, how can you keep that from happening?

Do you even know what your joy is? What makes you feel good inside? First, figure that one out, then make sure to protect it. If it makes you smile, glow and energizes others, protect it. You will be tested by the ones who are not accepting of it. Your shine is not for everyone so protect it for the ones who deserve it. Don't let anyone steal your joy because someone out there is waiting for it.

365

JULY 11TH

Are you happy with you? Do you feel good about yourself? I mean, on the inside? How is your spirit, your soul, this is where you need to start. Your spirit and soul must be in the right place for peace.

Peace is a part of happiness
and happiness comes from inner peace.

You must make sure to take time out every day to work on you. Make sure you are giving everything you can through the happiness that comes from the inside.

What an awesome feeling it is to be at peace and happy with who you are.

365

JULY 12ᵀᴴ

How do you start your day; a cup of coffee, exercise, meditation, reading?

We all have something or some way to start the day. It's important to take a little time in the morning to balance yourself for the day. If, your goal is to give your best, you must be your best.

Find that something that can help you start your day off right. How you start your day can play a major part in how it wraps up.

POSITIVE THOUGHTS, POSITIVE VIBES!

194

365

JULY 13TH

How do we attract positive energy? It's not always easy but it's all about perception.

Learn to see the positive in any situation. Let go of your perceived control or the need to be in control.

We all have the ability to allow positive energy within. I mean seriously, who really wants to live in negativity? Put yourself in positive situations, around positive people, think positively and let your light shine.

POSITIVE THOUGHTS, POSITIVE VIBES!

365

JULY 14$\underline{^{TH}}$

People spend so much time worried about the future. It's something that we really don't have any control over.

Instead of worrying about the future, why not create it? Play your part in positively creating the change you want to see now. That will lead into the future. Get up and start doing what you can in order to see the results you want. Tomorrow is not promised but we all have hope to see the sunrise in the morning.

Yes, tomorrow is a new day and you can start working on that right now.

365

JULY 15TH

It is often said, "Tomorrow is not promised and today is short." It is easier said than done to focus on today and not think about tomorrow.

We spend most of our time planning for the future and not enjoying the blessings we have today. In the blink of an eye, your world can turn upside down.

Today is the day. Love more, live more and pray more. Hold no regrets because what God has in store for tomorrow is not yours to control. He has given you today to see your blessings.

365

JULY 16$^{\underline{TH}}$

My father used to say, "You can't see unless you turn on the light."

We all have a switch and an opportunity to turn on our light. Allow your inner light to see you through the dark times.

Illuminate your path with positivity and your light will also shine for others.

TROUBLES DON'T LAST FOREVER
AND YOUR LIGHT IS ALWAYS THERE.

POSITIVE THOUGHTS, POSITIVE VIBES!

JULY 17<u>TH</u>

What does it mean to feel safe? Is it the ability to be yourself completely without judgement? This can be very difficult because the world is full of judgement.

Planet fitness says it best:
"Welcome to the judgement free zone."

Put yourself around people and in environments that will accept you for you.

When you feel good about yourself, the world is getting your best. Family, friends will see and feel your spirit and accept the true you. As we continue to grow and accept ourselves, we tend to judge others less and show more acceptance.

365

JULY 18ᵀᴴ

Maybe now is the opportunity for you to take a step back and take care of you. Look within, take a moment to fine tune yourself! Take a moment just to be at peace with yourself, love yourself and accept the beautiful person you are.

It's growth mode season and some doors are about to open for you. Clear out some of the old for some really good new. This will help attract the right person or persons to be in your space. People come into our lives at just the right time. Embrace the energy they give and allow that to enhance you on your journey.

365

JULY 19TH

I had a great conversation yesterday with a good friend of mine and could not stop laughing. You know that slump over almost falling to the ground laughing? BeBe Winans said it best, "Laughter is Just like Medicine." We all need to have the kind of moments when the laughing never stops. Laughing will help get you through the tough times. You know, those times when you are not feeling supported, or your heart is broken, or you just cannot find your smile, kind of day. Take your medicine and get your laugh on, my friends. It's the perfect medicine that will make your mind, body and soul feel good.

365

JULY 20TH

God is waiting for you to make the first step. Fannie Lou Hamer said it best, "You can pray until you faint, but unless you get up and try to do something, God's not gonna put it in your lap." That is the truth!

Today is the day of change, by making the first step he will put positive people in your pathway to help with the others. No need to hold back on the opportunity for positivity to take control. Your mind, body and soul are focused on seeing the change, and now it takes all of us working together to create it!

365

JULY 21ST

Why do we feel so connected to the beach? Being around water gives our brains a chance to rest and has a positive effect on our soul. The sun soaking on your skin releases those feel-good chemicals throughout your body.

My good friend Jackie Bieber says, "There's just something about the waves, the size of the ocean and how small we are. Even the salty air and the breeze, just completely restores and refreshes my soul"

Warm sand, gentle waves and soothing ambiance there is simply no better place to let go of daily stress than heading to the beach.

JULY 22ND

We spend so much time trying to change people or hoping they will be more like us.

You cannot change the people around you, but you can change the people you choose to be in your circle. Understanding ourselves better will allow our spirit to attract the right people to be in our space. If someone wants to change it will be up to them to do so.

Focus on fine tuning you, which will open the doors for the right people to walk in. It's all about the energy you give out and watch what comes back in.

365

JULY 23RD

Take yourself to a place of peace; a place where the wind blows and animals roam. It's a place that's far away from the hustle and bustle of the everyday chaos. It is where the living is easy and the thoughts have time to collect.

TODAY IS YOUR DAY TO FIND YOUR PEACE.

What makes your mind rest and your heart sing? You owe it to yourself to have that experience, if not forever, at least for a short moment.

365

JULY 24TH

There is a reason that you are still here. What does being still here really mean?

Your thoughts, beliefs, dreams and vision of the life you want are still here. They are still in the present waiting for you to start living. Are you stuck? Stuck in the "what if" zone?

Get up and start living. Put that plan in place and move forward. Leave those troubles behind and put your positive hat on. Step out into the world, today.

YOUR TIME IS NOW!

365

JULY 25TH

They say home is where the heart is. My oldest son, Carter, will ask "Daddy, what are we doing today?" I answer, "Not sure, what would you like to do?" He replies, "Stay home."

There is a comfort in being in the space you call home. It is a place where you feel love, safe and at peace.

Many of us search all of our lives looking for a place we can call home. Sometimes, the space is right in front of you. The simplicity of it is what we should look for.

HOME IS WHERE THE HEART IS SO LET YOUR HEART BE AT HOME.

365

JULY 26<u>TH</u>

There will be times when being alone is a good thing. Withdraw yourself from toxic people and situations. Allow your spirit some blessing time to rejuvenate your soul.

We go through stages in life where we need to find ourselves again. Look within to see who the real you is and if you're ok with that.

Alone time will let you revisit your inner self and focus on more positivity in your life.

POSITIVE THOUGHTS, POSITIVE VIBES!

365

JULY 27TH

What's already downstream is past you. Sometimes in life, we need to slow down and allow things to unfold.

Following the wrong things or wrong people can lead you down a path of uncertainty. Your heart will never fail you and living your best life is what you need to strive for. Most people just exist, and don't take the opportunity to live.

Take a moment to breathe and listen to the sounds around you. The rain can be soothing, just like a trickling stream or the ocean. The waves can provide a simple sounding board that will keep you on the right path.

365

JULY 28ᵀᴴ

We all control the type of life we want to live. Most of us would love to live a happy life filled with positivity.

Of course, there will be some bumps in the road, but our choices decide that. Also, things you have no control of will try to consume you. You decide what gets in the way of your happiness.

Take a few minutes every morning to balance yourself with positive thoughts that will keep you on the right path. Remember, you have the power to live the life you want.

365

JULY 29<u>TH</u>

Do people change? Do they offer their true selves or is it a façade? Yes, people change, and sometimes we never really know who they are.

Everyone is different and some people never show their true colors. They say some of us are an open book. We allow you to fully understand who and what we are. Change is in the eye of the beholder.

If change is true, then let it be, but if not, then the truth will come through. If not, then maybe you never really got their true spirit. Either way you will find out.

365

JULY 30TH

You had your life all planned out and it's not looking anything like you imagined. Married, kids, successful job, big house, fancy car, etc.... The issue is, you were moving too fast.

Remember that living in the now is always the best because we cannot predict the future. When we move too fast we forget to see all of the awesome things around us now.

You have the power to control the present which might help with the future. Live, love and enjoy what you have now and allow that positive energy to lead you into the future.

365

JULY 31ST

Nope, not a vacation to an exotic island with beautiful blue water. Get away from the negativity from within. The energy you have on the inside can be eating away at your very soul. It's not allowing you to breathe and swim your way through the waves. Negative thoughts, words and people are keeping you from your positive self. That's right. It is time to get away, so you can see the ocean from afar.

AUGUST 1ST

I hear you. You're not asking for much, maybe a nice dinner, little glass of wine, back rub. You've had a long day and those feet of yours are tired. Sometimes we're not surrounded by that special someone that can offer those things.

But it's important that you find a little time for self-care. Your mental and physical health allows you to take care of all the things needed. Put aside a few things today, take a moment to meditate, read a book, pour your own glass of wine or take a nice walk.

POSITIVE THOUGHTS, POSITIVE VIBES!

365

AUGUST 2ND

How cool is it that you have a happy place? Yes, we all need one. A place that provides peace in the midst of the storm. They call it 'Stormy Monday' as we all wait for Friday to come. That is not the way to live. We should love every day. Be able to enjoy the blessings of each day God gives us. Maybe you can transfer some of the awesome things about your happy place into day-to-day living. Peace can be found all around us if we just look for it. Push the negativity aside and allow happiness within yourself.

365

AUGUST 3ᴿᴰ

They say it's all in the eyes! They reveal our mood, feelings and even emotions. Eyes can convey a warm, bright and inviting positive vibe that touches the soul.

There is kindness in your eyes and you need to share it. It's like a warm subtle flame of goodness and trust. Through your eyes a glow appears that releases positive vibes, the ones that can heal, replenish and provide a safe space. The energy from the inside exudes through your beautiful eyes, providing a sense of peace. Just for second the negativity of the world vanishes away.

365

AUGUST 4ᵀᴴ

We all go through hard times but if we're prayerful and patient enough we will get through it. Stepping away or stepping aside can allow enough time to see a little light.

I know the road is not so smooth right now but like the pastor said "you have a friend in the Lord." Take a moment and allow him to order your steps. He can help you see the situation from a different perspective. Trouble don't last always, keep stirring things up, moving forward. The pot holes, detours and road blocks all have to be fixed at some point.

Glad to see you moving
in the right direction.

365

AUGUST 5TH

EMPOWERING YOUNG MINDS WITH POSITIVE VIBES!

Our "Positive Vibes for Kids" books are designed to ignite a spark of inspiration and positivity in the hearts of young readers. Each book features vibrant illustrations and powerful affirmations that nurture self-belief and a growth mindset.

Don't have any children in your life? Donate one to a school, library or even your church. Maybe a neighbor has children or maybe there is a little library box in your community? This is a great way to share the positive vibes!

POSITIVE THOUGHTS, POSITIVE VIBES!

218

365

AUGUST 6TH

FINDING PEACE IS NOT EASY.

Sometimes, the ones around you can take away your peace. If that is the case, it may behoove you to lose communication with some of those around you. It may be easier said than done, but the benefit will be a great reward.

Getting rid of the noise is the first step, which will allow the positive to come through. Too much negativity will not allow enough room for the positivity to move on in. Remember that peace begins from within. If your inside is not free of negativity, how can there be peace?

365

AUGUST 7<u>TH</u>

Trust the you from within. Tap in and understand who you are and what you will become. Things happen for a reason, things happen at a time and place when least expected.

We are all traveling a road where there is unknown. Trust your gut, and understand the road is long, but good. Yes there will be a few bumps here and there but being true to yourself will help lead you in the right direction.

The good in you will be good enough and the ride will be worth it in the end.

365

AUGUST 8TH

I was sitting here wondering why I don't look the same. I've changed! That's what it is, everything deep down inside feels a little different, my talk, walk and outlook on life. My smile is a little wider, my soul feels a little better and everyone says I'm wearing a glow. You know why? I took some time to focus on me. That's right, me!

Many of us spend so much time pleasing others that we forget about ourselves. Call it what you want, self-care, self-love… Create those boundaries and take care of 'you' for a change. Now you know why you don't look the same.

365

AUGUST 9<u>TH</u>

God gives us 24 hours, well maybe 12-16, to work. But it is still not enough to get everything done. Why do you have so many things to do? Why do we stress ourselves out with no relief, just to live?

Make a list of all the things you need to get done. Eliminate the ones that can wait until tomorrow and allow some time to relax. We must take time to be still and breathe. This provides the balance necessary to get all of those things done. Remember what you don't get done today will be there tomorrow and sometimes it's just not meant to get done.

365

AUGUST 10TH

Practice what you preach. Talk is cheap. Actions speak louder than words. The list goes on but you know what I'm trying to say. Be You! We spend so much time trying to please everyone else, hoping everyone is happy with what we're offering. Just make sure you offer the true you. If you believe in you then your actions will speak loudly and clearly.

Be the person that you want the world to know. Don't be afraid if someone will like it or not.

Not everyone will feel your spirit. Let your actions speak louder than their words!

AUGUST 11TH

You know what? I'm not sure I know what I want. I mean, what is life all about? What is the life I want to live? Maybe it's the life I'm living.

Did I miss it? Life might be pretty good right now? I like my job, my kiddos are great, I'm breathing, clothes on my back, etc. You know what? I think I like "this life right now." It's pretty darn good once you take a step back and appreciate all the wonderful things you have.

POSITIVE THOUGHTS, POSITIVE VIBES!

365

AUGUST 12TH

Yes, the feeling is REAL! Your heart feels like it has been torn into pieces, how do you reclaim it? You loved so hard that you lost yourself in the process. You forgot what you liked, loved and the person that shined on the inside. Everyone loved your smile and they wonder where did it go? The extraordinary person is still hanging out inside of you. Just trapped, but today you got those juices flowing. The negative energy that is consuming you is making its way out. It looks like you even have a new step, singing an old tune that makes your heart sing. Getting back into your groove feels real, so take back what is yours and allow those positive feelings to guide you.

AUGUST 13TH

Sometimes you can love someone deeply, and not really like them. In a world filled with many different personalities we are bound to need space from people.

Once you are able to breathe, you can find yourself feeling different about the person. Taking time to understand the relationship you have with that person is key.

You might not need to like the ones you love or love the ones you like all of the time. Letting it just be, could be the best thing.

365

AUGUST 14ᵀᴴ

What are you stressing about? You have done all that you can and given your best. Not much more can be done. This means there is no need to keep stressing.

We all have fifty million things to do with very little time. Maybe you need to minimize the things on your list or prioritize and put the most important things at the top.

I can tell you one thing: stress will not help. It blocks your mind and your ability to get things done.

AUGUST 15TH

I love seeing people happy. Laughing, singing and even dancing. You know when you're in the grocery store and you walk down that aisle and they're playing your favorite song and there you go. You're picking up your favorite cereal box while singing that tune. It's almost like no one is watching. You're living in the moment, enjoying the little things without thinking.

That's what being happy is all about. Laugh, sing and dance whenever possible, living in the moment is the best kind of medicine.

365

AUGUST 16TH

NATIONAL TELL A JOKE DAY

What did the coffee say to the tea?

"You may steep in your worries,
but I'm brewing up some good vibes!"

DOESN'T IT FEEL GOOD TO LAUGH?

I love seeing people laugh so hard, they hit the floor. You may have been through some challenging times, but you are living your best life and your laugh says it all.

AUGUST 17ᵀᴴ

Your passion will take you to places you have never been before. When you allow it to take over, nothing and no one can hold you back.

To some, it may be work or a chore but to you, it is you. The things you are passionate about order your steps in the direction of happiness. What you feel inside is like nothing else. To be honest, it's sometimes hard to even put it into words.

Passion is a beautiful thing that lives in all of us, it's time to let your passion shine!

365

AUGUST 18TH

Dance like no one is watching.
Love like there is no tomorrow.

Love comes from the heart which affects the mind, body and soul. We all love something or someone in our life time.

How we interpret, accept and/or run from it is up to us. Love what you do and feel the passion.

Believe in yourself and give your all or you may never know the possibilities. Give of yourself and enjoy the happiness of loving.

AUGUST 19TH

Does anyone really win or lose in life? What would you consider winning? Lots of money, fancy car, big house, lots of friends? Some people get lost in trying to win at life. They forget to live and appreciate what life has to offer through the process. Happiness comes in many forms but we know it starts from within.

A positive spirit can lead you to the happiness you seek. You could be winning right now and not even know it. Take a step back, breathe and feel the good all around you. You look like a winner to me.

AUGUST 20TH

Look in the mirror and appreciate the beautiful person that you see. You are amazing just the way you are. Always be confident in yourself and trust in your abilities. Believe that you can achieve anything that you set your mind to.

When you focus on the good and you allow the positive vibes to come in, you are capable of doing great things.

KEEP SMILING AND KEEP SHINING.

365

AUGUST 21ˢᵀ

I always emphasize the importance of surrounding yourself with positive people—those who energize, inspire, and encourage you to be your best self.

In this circle, there's no room for jealousy because these individuals see the beauty in your growth and genuinely want you to keep evolving so you can share your best self with the world.

Take a look at your circle and ensure that those around you are truly part of your 'vibe tribe'!

365

AUGUST 22<u>ND</u>

We are all blessed with our own voice, a gift, and a story to tell. Share it. More importantly, listen. Listen without condition, without ego.

Is there something you have always wanted to do? Don't allow negative energy to hold you back from doing it.

SEIZE THE MOMENT!

You have the power to positively impact the world. Look deep down into your soul and let your light shine. Reflect.

SOMEONE IS WAITING FOR YOU!

365

AUGUST 23ᴿᴰ

We all have a story.

Most of it comes from past experiences or simply the past. Our parents and grand-parents share their stories which help mold and shape us. But, the here and now plays an important role in our current story.

We have the ability to reshape what the next chapter will be. We might not know the ending but the pathway we choose can lead us to a positive ending.

365

AUGUST 24TH

Should we just be focused on our own needs and not the needs of others? Within this universe of ours we find different ways to connect or disconnect. It doesn't matter where you come from, who you are or where you are going; we all need to connect.

When you let your light shine, it allows others to connect. When you open yourself up, you give others permission to explore the true you. That's when the connection begins, and where it leads can be a positive mystery.

365

AUGUST 25TH

Be the smile you want to see,
be the love you want to feel.

We all have the ability to bring a little
sunshine into the world. Your attitude and
approach on life can make or break your
whole day. So bring an attitude of gratitude.

The energy we give is the energy we will
receive. Your light tells the world that
positivity is within. This will drive out the
negative energy and fill your spirit with the
love it needs.

365

AUGUST 26TH

There is an old saying, "Home is where the heart is." This can have so many meanings and it really depends on how you want to interpret it. Is it the place you feel safe, loved and/or at peace? Is it the physical house you live in or that special place you go to reconnect? Or, is it that special someone you are willing to move around the world with because you feel at home with them?

In this crazy world, just knowing where home is, is very important. Allow your soul to feed your heart and that will provide peace in whatever you feel is your home. Let your heart rest and regenerate.

365

AUGUST 27TH

Trust your heart and it will never steer you wrong. The mind may play tricks on you but the heart never will. Yes, the road you travel will be bumpy, allowing a few scars along the way. These are the not-so-pleasant times of your past.

If you trust your heart, follow it. More than likely, the outcome will be what was meant to be. Let that light of yours shine and allow your heart to tell your story. The world is ready for what your heart has to offer.

365

AUGUST 28ᵀᴴ

Take a moment today—and every day—to let the people in your life know how much you appreciate them. Send a message, a note, make a quick phone call, or surprise them with a thoughtful gift.

Celebrate the goodness these people bring to your life and to the world. Thank you all for joining us in this Positive Vibes movement. I appreciate each and every one of you for spreading kindness, love, and positive energy.

AUGUST 29ᵀᴴ

Just because it works for you doesn't mean it will work for someone else. We all have our own road and journey to travel. It's hard enough to make our own life changes so trying to help or guide others can be difficult.

Our changes come at the right time and we have to be in the right space to accept them. Someone else might not be there yet. So, when offering advice and suggestions to others, take that into consideration. Change comes in all forms and someone else's change might not be yours to handle.

AUGUST 30TH

Take a look in the mirror, don't you look fabulous? Of course, you do. You are an amazing, loving, caring and giving person.

It's so important to take moment and look in the mirror and say I'm a beautiful, awesome person. I'm strong, kind, free spirited, and accepting. Yes, accepting of who I am now, and the continued growth which is fine-tuning this amazing person that I see in the mirror.

AUGUST 31ST

How do we go through the healing process? When is it time to recognize that there are things within you that need healing in order to move forward? What does the healing process look like? Is this something that you can do alone, or is this something that takes help from others? The first step is, recognizing that you're hurt or something is damaged within that needs healing. You really can't put a timetable on how long it will take for you to go through this process but recognizing it is the biggest thing. You will travel on your journey with stumbling blocks, pitfalls and detours. When the time is right for you, the healing process will take place.

365

SEPTEMBER 1ST

Living within our universe and painting the picture we show the world will create a canvas filled with different colors blending into one story. Your story!

We all have a picture to paint and hopefully the world will accept it. If not, remember God has a plan just for you. You are the painter and your story needs to be shared. Someone, somewhere will see, hear and feel who and what you are.

The connection with those will honor your pathway that God has planned for you.

POSITIVE THOUGHTS, POSITIVE VIBES!

365

SEPTEMBER 2ND

Every time I turn around, God continues to bless me. I pause and recognize all that I have around me. It's so important to take a step back and recognize all the wonderful things that you have; health, family, home, car and of course some peace. Moving forward, growing, learning and soaking in all the good the world has to offer.

Through this, the blessings will continue. Some might be big, and most will be very small. Some of us are always looking for the big things and we miss out on the little ones. Thank you, Lord, for giving me an open mind so I can accept and recognize the blessings.

365

SEPTEMBER 3RD

You have the power to choose what your attitude is. You can alter your life by changing your attitude. Your outlook and perception can not only impact you but also the people you connect with.

Is your attitude worth catching? If not, how can you tap in and make sure what you give is what you want to receive.

Maintaining a positive attitude is not always easy, but it can be done.

POSITIVE THOUGHTS, POSITIVE VIBES!

365

SEPTEMBER 4ᵀᴴ

The great outdoors! My youngest son loves being outside. He finds joy in everything from catching bugs to looking for slugs late at night. Being outdoors makes him happy. God's little creatures can offer a sense of gratification. Go take a walk or sit on the porch.

Take a few minutes to enjoy the peacefulness of the outdoors. It's simplistic, with no drama or over thinking. Nature allows you to just be and enjoy what it has to offer. You might be surprised how good it makes your spirit feel.

365

SEPTEMBER 5TH

As you grow and discover more of who you are, you naturally attract people who uplift and inspire you.

You are worthy of love, light, and positive connections that help you become the truest, most extraordinary version of yourself. Discover the you that is waiting to shine.

POSITIVE THOUGHTS, POSITIVE VIBES!

365

SEPTEMBER 6TH

We all have a name but what does yours mean to you? Your name can mean so many things to you and the ones you're connected to. Does it define who you are? Will people remember your name in the way you want?

You have the ability to shape what your name means to you and the world. We are all given a name to be proud of and to share with others. Our names connect us in ways we can't sometimes explain.

Allow the known and unknown of who you are to be a positive impact on others, through a name given by God.

365

SEPTEMBER 7TH

God only gives us one life. What do you plan to do with yours? Don't spend most of the day complaining or thinking about the negativity.

Get your butt up and start living. Live for you first and the rest shall follow. Life doesn't have to be that difficult.

Do what's right, treat people fairly and laugh as much as you can. There is nothing more beautiful to hear than the laughter from a child. Remember that as you plan out your life.

Laugh like a child
and live like there is no tomorrow.

365

SEPTEMBER 8TH

TODAY IS YOUR DAY TO BE KIND.

A single act of kindness can have a positive rippling effect. Share of yourself and the next person may share with someone else. People talk about karma. What we do now, can come back to affect us later.

It's not about being self-absorbed but rather, giving of yourself which will allow a peaceful spirit to take over. Being kind frees your spirit and unlocks the chains and negativity.

365

SEPTEMBER 9TH

Are you running low on fumes or on empty? Do the daily tasks of the week have you feeling spent?

What will you do to rejuvenate your mind, body and soul? At the end of the day, you can only do what you can do.

Don't continue to run low on fumes and burn out. Stop and listen to your body and get those juices flowing again.

THE WORLD NEEDS THE BEST YOU HAVE TO OFFER!

365

SEPTEMBER 10TH

How you live or choose to live will be how people view you. It's not about how much money you make or anything with material value. It lies within the character of the person you are.

You hear it often... he or she would give the shirt off their back, or, he or she always had a kind word to say.

Your positive impact will have a lasting effect on every person you meet. Let that be your legacy - one of giving, and less of receiving.

SEPTEMBER 11TH

Most of us spend our time trying to live a perfect life. Or, might I say trying to fit in with the latest styles, home, car, the list goes on. When seeking the perfect life doesn't work, some turn to drugs, alcohol and other toxic devices. Just find a way to live your life.

GOD HAS A LIFE JUST FOR YOU!

The journey is yours and not everyone or everything is meant to be in it. Be you! Love the life you have and continue to add positive things to it. It will be an awesome feeling when you feel good about you!

SEPTEMBER 12ᵀᴴ

You know that special someone, the one that ignites something in us that no one else has ever done? It doesn't have to be romantic, just a powerful conversation.

There is always a reason why someone comes into our lives at a certain time. They're giving you the ability to feel deep down inside your soul. These types of relationships help us with growth. They give us the ability to feel, give and have a glimpse of what love feels like. Those types of relationships provide the teachable moments, which will help us with future connections.

365

SEPTEMBER 13TH

POSITIVE THINKING DAY

Today is a reminder that our mindset has the power to shape our world. When we choose to focus on the good, embrace challenges as opportunities, and believe in the possibility of growth, we unlock our true potential.

So, let's fill today with optimism, gratitude, and the belief that we can overcome anything with the right mindset.

POSITIVE THOUGHTS, POSITIVE VIBES!

365

SEPTEMBER 14TH

How important is it to you to find your path? Our purpose in life is something most of us want to understand. Should we spend most of our time searching for this? Will we stumble on it by accident?

Making peace with yourself, accepting yourself and believing from within is key. Live your life and your path will be what it will be. Your view of the present will offer a positive outlook on the future.

POSITIVE THOUGHTS, POSITIVE VIBES!

365

SEPTEMBER 15TH

Everyone has talent. God gives us all some type of gift. Sometimes we will allow stumbling blocks to divert us off our path.

It is not always easy to analyze yourself to see and feel what your gift might be. Take a moment to think about your skills, abilities and passions.

The talent that has been bestowed upon you is waiting to be unleashed. No stress, just breathe and feel.

POSITIVE THOUGHTS, POSITIVE VIBES!

365

SEPTEMBER 16TH

Don't let anyone or anything change what you feel is true to you. God gave you a voice, your voice to share with the world. Some will interpret it as good, some not so good or, maybe just different.

If what you offer is your truth then that is good enough. The doubt brings faith and the faith brings hope. Love the life you have and keep living it. Through your truth, you will grow.

POSITIVE THOUGHTS, POSITIVE VIBES!

365

SEPTEMBER 17ᵀᴴ

We all have something that we really want to have or achieve. Whether it is personal, business or pleasure, if you really want it, you can get it.

Take a moment to write down why it's so important to you and how it makes you feel. It could be obtainable sooner or later and it can be difficult to wait.

Sometimes good things come to those who wait. Patience is a virtue. We have heard these things time and time again. Think of them as you move forward in achieving what you want and continue to move forward.

365

SEPTEMBER 18ᵀᴴ

I left saying, "WOW! That was awesome, amazing just the best." My spirit felt so good and I'm leaving with so much positive juice flowing though me…

You're probably wondering, where was I just now? I just had some amazing conversation, that's it. Great conversation with someone who's spirit has the same energy. You know that feeling when you don't want the conversation to end? Yup, that's what it was, some amazing conversation. Let's keep those juices flowing.

365

SEPTEMBER 19ᵀᴴ

Some might say you woke up this morning on the wrong side of the bed. Are your plans just not working out the way you want them to?

When things are going wrong, what do you do? Throw in the towel or turn a negative into a positive?

Look at the small things and start there. You might be able to take care of a few little things to get your day going. Challenges can be chances for you to view things differently.

Taking a different perspective could turn your day around. There is a reason for everything; take a step back and breathe.

365

SEPTEMBER 20TH

What is your purpose in life? It's a question that can feel hard to answer. But your purpose often lies in your passion. What excites you? Today is the perfect day to explore that. Whether it's gardening, design, cooking, exercise, or something else, find what makes you feel alive.

Your purpose comes from following your passion and sharing your gifts with the world. The answer lies within you. Most people spend their lives doing what they don't love—don't be one of them. Passion is the key to happiness and to turning your dreams into reality. Embrace what you love, and let it guide you forward.

365

SEPTEMBER 21ST

Share a genuine, heartfelt Happy Sunday, my friends! And if it isn't Sunday, look forward to it.

Share a genuine, heartfelt smile, radiating positive energy that brings light to the world—something we all need to see and feel.

We each have something special to offer; let today and every day be an opportunity to spread a little positivity and enjoy the beauty it brings from within.

365

SEPTEMBER 22ND

Fall is upon us! The trees are different sizes, and bare different colors. As we enjoy the beauty of it all, it puts things in perspective.

Our community is a melting pot of all different shades. We all blend together to form one. No matter where you came from or where you are going, we are all part of one universe.

POSITIVE THOUGHTS, POSITIVE VIBES!

Proverbs 27:19

*As water reflects the face,
so one's life reflects the heart.*

365

SEPTEMBER 23RD

Today and always, may positive things fill your life. Weed out the negative and replace it with the positive.

When you let your light shine you have the opportunity to bless someone else. The energy we release will invite positivity into your life and also add something to someone else's.

As you face those challenges today,
may your light shine brightly.

POSITIVE THOUGHTS, POSITIVE VIBES!

365

SEPTEMBER 24TH

I see you flying, I mean, soaring along in life. They say some birds are not meant to be caged. Your feathers are just too bright and there is a little bit of an ambitious, spontaneous side about you. Not everyone gets you or understands the way you walk and talk. It's on a whole different vibration; you groove and move different from the rest. It's beautiful when you get it. I mean, get who you are and what your purpose in life is. You share your gifts and allow the world to experience your spirit just the way God gave it to you. Surround yourself with the people who see it too, and your feathers will continue to grow, and the beauty of your spirit shall shine.

365

SEPTEMBER 25TH

National One-Hit Wonder Day

I remember back in college when Mark Morrison's Return of the Mack hit the airwaves—one of the greatest one-hit wonders ever! I'm sure many of you can recall a favorite artist or create your own list of unforgettable one-hit wonders.

So, on National One-Hit Wonder Day, let's celebrate those iconic songs from the past that still bring us joy.

POSITIVE THOUGHTS, POSITIVE VIBES!

365

SEPTEMBER 26TH

There's something incredibly powerful about a hug from someone who truly cares about you. Today might be the perfect day to give a hug or ask for one from that special person.

They say the longer the hug the more it has healing properties. So, hug each other... but know when to let go as well. It is about being in-tune with those around you.

POSITIVE THOUGHTS, POSITIVE VIBES!

365

SEPTEMBER 27ᵀᴴ

We all have our own journey. The question is, are you living your best life?

It's important that we focus on the simple things in life allowing us to travel a road with fewer bumps and potholes.

We tend to get caught up in the concept of what will make us happy; a nice car, a big house and trying to keep up with the Jones's. But does that *really* make us happy?

Start from within and focus on the little things. It will put you on the pathway of living your best life.

365

SEPTEMBER 28ᵀᴴ

Enjoy life's simple pleasures. That includes a nice cup of coffee, a morning sunrise, and a cool summer breeze. We are blessed when we can recognize those simple pleasures.

The world gets us going. It's like a rat race and we're always on the go. We start to focus on the big things or so-called things of the future. Today is your day to live. Make a step forward, maybe take a step back. Or, just stop moving and be still. Maybe make a 360 degree turn and take in all of the simple pleasures around you.

Positive things are in front of you and you need to take a moment and breathe in it.

365

SEPTEMBER 29TH

NATIONAL COFFEE DAY

My day always starts with a nice cup of coffee. On National Coffee Day, choose your favorite flavor—hazelnut, French vanilla, or classic black. Whatever your choice, a fresh cup in the morning is a great way to start the day on the right foot.

The aroma of fresh coffee while you sit on your deck is a perfect, positive way to set the tone for your day and create the atmosphere you want as you move forward.

365

SEPTEMBER 30TH

To me, "Love me today, leave me tomorrow," sounds like a sad old song. Not today! Figure out if your love and friendship is true.

You can be sure; I will not be the same person you left. My heart is big and it's here for you, but the back and forth is not working anymore. Enough is enough. My mind, body and soul deserve to have positive energies for someone or something that is true. So today I'm taking care of me and making sure I'm in the right space. Keep it real or keep it moving.

365

OCTOBER 1ST

Each day, you rise with courage and determination, embracing your journey and honoring the strength that lives within you.

You are unique, and your spirit shines brightly, even when the road feels unfamiliar.

Today arise with the knowledge that you have this! This day is yours to live.

POSITIVE THOUGHTS, POSITIVE VIBES!

365

OCTOBER 2ND

This might sound a little strange, but there's something unique about being fully immersed in your own thoughts. Having enough quiet time to reflect and contemplate whatever you choose can be profoundly grounding.

There's a sense of peace that comes when the mind is free to wander, without having to focus on any one thing. It's as if the thoughts are allowed to float and settle in a way that brings clarity and sustainability. Our thoughts hold significant emotional and spiritual power over us, so I hope that being in the midst of your own brings you a sense of peace, even if just for a moment.

365

OCTOBER 3RD

Life is happening. If you let life happen without you, you won't be the only one who suffers. You're probably thinking, *what the heck does he mean?* Let me explain. When there are so many good things going on, I mean one after the next, and you miss them, you miss out.

Maybe you feel like you're about to explode and it's hard to stay present. It's got you all over the place even looking into the future for what is next. It's the perfect time to sit back and soak it in.

Yes, it's happening and without a negative vibe in the air.

365

OCTOBER 4TH

Sometimes the world gets too big and we have to figure out ways to break it down so we can handle it. Sometimes it's difficult to just breathe. Find a way to keep it simple.

A quote from my favorite movie *Shawshank Redemption*, "The world went and got itself in a big hurry."

Find a way to slow down, see the world a little smaller, and allow the enormity of it all to slow down and simplify.

POSITIVE THOUGHTS, POSITIVE VIBES!

OCTOBER 5TH

Dr. Martin Luther King Jr said it best, "Darkness cannot drive out darkness; only light can do that. Hate cannot drive out hate; only love can do that." Our ability to forgive is something we consistently need to work on. Forgiveness is not easy; you have to allow yourself to be vulnerable in some situations. Without forgiveness, there is no peace!

In life, we will have to forgive in order to move forward. Not only do you free yourself when you let go of the past, but you live in the now! When you take a step back to see the big picture, you understand the importance of letting go and letting God lead!

365

OCTOBER 6ᵀᴴ

THE WORLD IS ALWAYS ON THE GO.

My father, being a landscaper,
often said, "Grass never sleeps."

New York City is often referred to as the city that never sleeps. The craziness of this world can have us spinning in circles.

It's not always easy to find time to even think. You must take some time out every day to be still. This will give you time to focus on your needs and not your wants.

Your priorities will align and your spirit will feel at ease.

365

OCTOBER 7TH

Your power lies on the inside. It's time for you to light that fire and allow your emotions to take you there. The "there" is fueling inside of you and waiting.

Use your emotions to change the way you feel, think, and act. Laugh a little. Sing a little. Maybe even pray a little. Use what God has given you to create the positive change you are seeking.

Nothing will happen until you let go and allow the power from within you to take control and process change.

OCTOBER 8TH

You call that person your friend who was once a stranger. You connected for a reason. How we view, interpret or accept the connection is up to us. We need to allow ourselves to be vulnerable and open to the unlimited possibilities of the connection.

We were all strangers at one point and allowed ourselves to feel, like, love and acquire a friendship with someone. Being open to the connection can take your mind, body and soul to new heights.

365

OCTOBER 9TH

Always remember the importance of you!

Every one of us plays an important role in creating history. Our lives will not only be shaped by our experiences, but the choices we make. The life you live continues to impact the ones around even if you don't recognize it.

Someone is watching, listening and taking in your light. Allow it to shine and never underestimate your possibilities of making a positive impact.

Walk, talk and live with a purpose for the importance of you is valuable to the world.

OCTOBER 10TH

I'm looking to be in the midst of peaceful situations and as many peaceful people as I can be around. It's not always easy to find peace in a world filled with so much noise. So, it's very important that we balance our lives and surround ourselves with peaceful oriented people.

You know, people who are in search of peace as well. The ones who are in continued growth mode, fine tuning themselves from within and letting go of the negative.

PROTECTING YOUR PEACE IS PRICELESS!

365

OCTOBER 11ᵀᴴ

You want to be loved and accepted but no one gets you. What? Are you that difficult to understand? You don't look like you're from outer space. The issue could be the people you're around. They say surround yourself with like-minded people. Folks that you have the same views and likes that you have.

Maybe by making a few adjustments, you might come across a few folks that 'get you'. If you're willing to open up it will get easier. The chances are more on the positive side of people seeing the real you.

365

OCTOBER 12TH

They say, "take the bull by the horns" and get it done. What are you waiting for? The time is now. You can get it done and get it done, now. Look deep down inside and find the will power to fight through.

Is it fear holding you back? The fear of the unknown? Fear will rob you of the excitement and joy that is waiting for you. Remember that God is always with you, and wants you to get it done. Nike said it best, "Just Do It." Even through failure, the growth will lead you into the positive outcome on the other side.

You must try and you must do You!

OCTOBER 13TH

TODAY IS THE DAY
WHEN YOU CAN CREATE CHANGE.

Sometimes we're put into situations that allow us to make a difference. Big or small, the opportunity has presented itself and it's up to you to take the leap.

A leap of faith into something that challenges your being and challenges your current thoughts into new ones can bring about change. Change will happen with you or without. Don't hold back on the opportunity of positivity.

365

OCTOBER 14ᵀᴴ

Knowing your worth allows you to tap into your everyday power and can change your life for the better. How do you take back control and appreciate your self-worth?

Put yourself around people who see you for the person you are. The willingness to look from within is a great start. Self-worth is defined as, "The sense of one's own value or worth as a person." Because God made you, this already shows your value and worth.

Don't let the negativity of the world steal that from you. Hold your head up, let go, breathe, and spend some time in the positive zone! Know your worth!

365

OCTOBER 15ᵀᴴ

Not sure where you're going or what your next stop is? Did you ask God to order your steps? Yes, the train is always moving but do you know what your next stop is?

Is life what you expected? Do you need more? Sometimes less is more and what you are searching for could be sitting right in front of you. Stop searching and moving around so much. Be still and breathe and allow the train to fuel up.

Running on fumes can cloud your pathway and put you on a road of uncertainty.

365

OCTOBER 16TH

There's a song that says,
"we're waiting on the world to change."

Well, I think the change is up to you. You have the power to create the change you want to see in your life. People will come and go and circumstances might just fuel you forward in making the much-needed change. Don't wait for tomorrow when today is right in front of you.

Who knows what tomorrow will bring, so if you feel the need now, then do it!

POSITIVE THOUGHTS, POSITIVE VIBES!

365

OCTOBER 17TH

Be the creator of the change you seek.

Michael Jackson said it best, "If you want to make the world a better place, take a look at yourself and make a change"

We all have the ability to create change whether big or small. Let's not look to our right or left but in front of the mirror and allow that person to create change.

POSITIVE THOUGHTS, POSITIVE VIBES!

Reference: *Line sung by* Michael Jackson *in the song "Man in the Mirror" written by Siedah Garrett and Glen Ballard, from the album* Bad, *1987*

365

OCTOBER 18$^{\underline{TH}}$

Everybody knows I love old R&B. I hear the Spinners "I'm working my way back to you babe." Sometimes it might be worth moving forward, right? Working your way back might not help you turn into the person you need to be today. I hear ya, that burning love inside, might not be at the right temperature or for the right person.

Take some time to work on you, fine tune the things and create the space needed for your present self. Something is burning inside of you and that is change, the change that will put you in some really good spaces. I see you putting a new spin on an old song, "working it your way."

365

OCTOBER 19ᵀᴴ

Mama told me the road wouldn't be easy. When the storm comes your way, ask yourself, "Are you ready to stand? Are you secure in yourself to know that this too shall pass?"

You will get through this just like you got through the last one. God never gives us more than we can handle. So, stand tall, and trust that He will bring you through.

THIS MEANS: HAVE FAITH!

Faith is the substance of things hoped for, and the evidence of things unseen.

365

OCTOBER 20TH

There's an old saying,
"God helps those that help themselves."

If you make the first step, He will make the second. So, what are you waiting for? They say money doesn't grow on trees, you have to go out and make it.

It's really easy to understand, you must take the lead. Send out that resume, organize the community clean up, start writing that book. Make the first step and then ask God to order your steps in the right direction.

YOU WON'T KNOW UNTIL YOU TRY!

OCTOBER 21ˢᵀ

They say time rules us all, and it often feels like there's never enough of it. The world moves so fast that finding a moment to breathe can seem nearly impossible.

We get caught up in the endless tasks, focusing on everything that needs fixing, and sometimes overlook the good things happening around us. Our perception of time can shape how we use it.

Take a step back, prioritize what truly matters each day, and always make room to breathe.

OCTOBER 22ᴺᴰ

Some days you feel like all is lost. You're buried in worries, troubles, bills and more. Well, it's time to sprinkle on some new soil and allow your flower to grow.

Find a new way to look at things or grow some new roots. Turn in some of the old for something new. Make a few new friends, change jobs, move into a new neighborhood.

A change of scenery can make all the difference in how you view yourself. Planting yourself in new soil can allow your flower to grow and change your current situation.

OCTOBER 23RD

Start living the life you have and not the one you had. It's in the past for a reason. Second chances are all about acceptance.

Understanding where you came from will lead you to where you are going. Moving forward is about growth. Love yourself enough to know your life is always evolving and it's best to be in the here and now.

THE OPPORTUNITY IS YOURS FOR THE TAKING.

POSITIVE THOUGHTS, POSITIVE VIBES!

365

OCTOBER 24ᵀᴴ

WHY IS IT IMPORTANT TO KEEP YOUR WORD?

The old saying, "Your word is your bond," is important. The promises you make, or the promises you break, define who you are and showcase the real you for the whole world to see.

Sometimes it's best to say, "No," than to promise something you can't fulfill. Not everyone can accept, "No," but they can respect your honesty.

Honesty is the best policy and the insurance it brings is priceless.

365

OCTOBER 25ᵀᴴ

You pray and pray but your situation is still the same. You ask God to answer your prayers but nothing is happening. Question? What are you praying for? If your prayer is answered is your soul ready to accept it? Sometimes we need to take a step back and be real about what we're asking God. Maybe order my steps so I can be ready to accept what You have for me.

Your prayer might not be his prayer for you. If you don't open yourself to seeing, you might just miss the little blessings He has all around you. God is ready to help cleanse your soul and have you on the right path made just for you.

365

OCTOBER 26ᵀᴴ

I just love the song by Champagne "how about us". Some people are made for each other. Some people can love one another for life. How about us? I love hearing the stories of couples who have been together 40 and 50 years.

I asked a question how do you do it? How do you stay together for so long? Most say living a simple life, communication, compromise and be true to yourself and your partner.

It's a beautiful thing to behold true love between two people, the love that can last through all kinds of weather.

365

OCTOBER 27TH

The word, "trust" may not be a friend of yours. What does it mean to trust or be trusted? We give of ourselves and have no choice but to trust. We have to trust in others, ourselves and the universe that some good will come from it.

But what happens when it doesn't? When the word trust is not too friendly? How do you trust again, repair and move forward? You do because moving forward is all you can do. Not everything or everyone is untrusting. The ups and downs are a part of life. Push the non-trusting aside today and keep it moving.

OCTOBER 28TH

NATIONAL CHOCOLATE DAY

Anyone who knows me knows that a piece of milk chocolate with almonds is my absolute favorite! Yes, I have a sweet tooth, and what better day to indulge than National Chocolate Day? Today is the perfect excuse to savor a bit of sweetness.

But as we celebrate, let's remember the joy of moderation—a small treat to honor the day while keeping balance in mind. Cheers to us, chocolate lovers!"

365

OCTOBER 29TH

Take care of your spirit to fuel your physical self. Your spiritual self is the most important component of your being. You must do things and surround yourself with people who energize your spirit. If your spirit feels good most times your body will follow.

Nutrition and exercise are very important as well. Balance yourself by getting your spirit in the right place. You need both your spiritual and physical self to be balanced so the world is getting the best of You!

365

OCTOBER 30TH

What are you afraid of? What is holding you back? Fear? Scared of failing? Most of us are scared, but when you look within, you have the power to overcome.

Make your determination to succeed stronger than your fears. If you don't try, you will never know your potential.

You control your ability to achieve and succeed. Remove the stumbling blocks, negative energy and give the world your best.

POSITIVE THOUGHTS, POSITIVE VIBES!

365

OCTOBER 31ST

How do you stare fear in the face? You have to look deep within and use your past experience to provide strength.

It's not easy to do or attempt something you fear. Taking the leap will not be easy but the outcome could be worth it.

You will never know what you can do unless you try. Through this process you will find out more about yourself. Build confidence in the old and new you.

POSITIVE THOUGHTS, POSITIVE VIBES!

365

NOVEMBER 1ST

NATIONAL AUTHOR'S DAY

As we continue through this Positive Vibes movement, many of you know my story—I never imagined I'd be the author of several affirmation books. On National Authors Day, I salute everyone who puts pen to paper to create something that will positively impact the world.

We all have a story to share. So, if you have one, don't hesitate to write it down, and feel free to reach out to us. Together, we can support one another, spread positive vibes, and impact the world in amazing ways.

NOVEMBER 2ND

I know how to GIVE! I am a very giving person. But what happens when you've given so much that you get burnt out? Today might be the day to take a step back and take some time out for you. It's not selfish to think about your well-being. You don't need anything in return. What you need is balance. Surround yourself with people who raise and lift you up. Sometimes the return is to take the time to rebalance, reorganize and rejuvenate yourself. Giving is important, but we can't burn ourselves out. They call it creating boundaries. Create some boundaries for yourself that will make sure you provide the balance that you need.

365

NOVEMBER 3RD

No one knows what you have been through or what you have seen. Whatever you have conquered, let it shine through your soul.

Allow your spirit to run free and the sparkle in your eyes to shine bright. You may never know the impact you will have on another.

When your soul smiles, you wear a glow that will attract positivity. You control what you allow in and out.

POSITIVE THOUGHTS, POSITIVE VIBES!

365

NOVEMBER 4TH

They say laughing is the best medicine.
Sometimes I laugh so hard that tears come
out of my eyes. Laughing makes your soul
feel good and sends positive energy to your
mind. I love people who tell jokes and laugh
at their own humor.

The ability to allow yourself to laugh is one
of the greatest gifts. Seek those opportunities
to let yourself go and take in the positive
energy laughing can offer.

POSITIVE THOUGHTS, POSITIVE VIBES!

NOVEMBER 5TH

Great leaders make sure to boost the morale of the ones around them.

If people believe in themselves, they appreciate what's in front of them. Leaders have to overcome obstacles, and the way they handle adversity shows the qualities of the type of leader they are.

We all have leadership abilities in us, we just have to find our pathway or calling. The task can be small or huge but don't allow YOU to stop yourself from accomplishing the impossible.

365

NOVEMBER 6TH

I woke up this morning and something said, "Listen to your gut!" What does it mean to listen to your gut?

Something deep down inside tells you that you're making the right move, and that you've found the right person. You feel like you've found the right way to go. Trust your gut and make that move.

Whether it turns out the way you expected or not, trust yourself. In our lives, we must find something or someone to trust. Look deep inside and go with it!

365

NOVEMBER 7TH

Fannie Mae Hamer said it best. She was tired of fighting a fight that seemed to be unwinnable. But she kept fighting.

You do the same thing day in and day out. What are you fighting for? A better life, family or just the ability to find peace? When we see the big picture, the fight is worth it. You will be tired and have times when you want to give up.

But today is not that day because the big picture tells you to press on. There is a light at the end of the tunnel.

365

NOVEMBER 8TH

You know what I did last night? I sat back, outside by my chimenea and gazed into the fire. Sitting by a nice fire and gazing upwards at the starry night gave me an opportunity to be at one with myself. It gave me an opportunity to relax and be present. Yes, being present is so important.

There is something about the off-rhythm crackle of the flames, that just by watching them, focuses your mind. What do you see? What do you feel when you stare into the fire? Is it a moment of peace to clear your mind and rebalance your soul? Let the fireside warm your spirit.

365

NOVEMBER 9TH

Is the ability to have inner peace important to you? If so, what does inner peace feel and look like? Feeling peaceful can sometimes be correlated to being at the beach. The sound of the waves, breeze and the sand in between your feet feel really peaceful.

Inner peace is important because it comes from within. The exterior will look and feel better with inner peace. The true happiness someone feels must come from within first to allow your positive light to shine on the outside.

NOVEMBER 10TH

I know, you keep getting knocked down. Every time you catch your breath, here comes something else. You ask yourself, when will it end?

Some might say life is never ending. There will always be someone to take care of or something to handle. Sounds like it's all about balance -- understanding what you can and cannot do.

Your limits are not limitations but an important warning to slow down. Your mind and body will speak to you. It is up to you to listen.

365

NOVEMBER 11TH

Why have you stopped growing? Most of us get stuck in what we know and not what we don't know. Benjamin Franklin said it best, "The doors of wisdom are never shut." There's always room for growth and always something to learn.

We tend to get comfortable in our lives and the daily grind, so we forget there is always something to learn. Growth comes from wanting to know the unknown. Yes, the unknown can be scary, but if you look from within, you can overcome the fear.

Your continued growth will take you places you can only dream of.

365

NOVEMBER 12TH

Your truth is NOW, not in the past nor future. Who are you? Who do you want to be? You must live and speak your truth.

Those who want to hear you, will listen. Others will try to silence you. Live, share and express who you are without limits. It will attract those you need in your life.

Let the thoughts from your mind flow through your heart and be true to your soul. Today is the day you live the life you have always wanted.

POSITIVE THOUGHTS, POSITIVE VIBES!

365

NOVEMBER 13TH

WORLD KINDNESS DAY

Today and every day, let kindness be the gift you give the world—you never know who might need it. On Happy World Kindness Day, reach out with a warm hug, share an encouraging word, or offer a gesture that reminds someone they are valued and loved.

Kindness is a force we can never have too much of, and the positive energy it creates helps lift us through life's challenges and brightens our celebrations of the joyful moments. Take a moment today to spread love and warmth. You might just make someone's day unforgettable.

365

NOVEMBER 14TH

The world has a funny way of loving us. It doesn't always show us our worth. You stumbled, tripped, or could barely hold yourself up. That's in the past, and today you're going through your growth and cleansing process and understand that God has a bigger plan for you. Your life is bigger than you, and once you start to understand your worth, you will understand your place along your journey.

We all make mistakes. We all have done things that, maybe, we're not so proud of, or happy about, but all of that is in the past and today you're living in the present.

365

NOVEMBER 15TH

As the holiday season surrounds us, it brings the perfect time to gather with loved ones—family and friends—who fill our hearts with joy.

This season is about more than gifts and festive meals; it's a moment to reflect on the blessings of the year and the wonderful people who make our lives richer. The holidays remind us to pause, give thanks, and share in the warmth of togetherness, creating memories that will last a lifetime.

May this season fill us with gratitude, love, and a renewed spirit of appreciation for all that we have and the people who make our lives brighter.

365

What are priorities? Things that are urgent can cloud our priorities. Nothing shapes us more than focusing on the need and not the want.

A person on their death bed sees the world differently. Understanding that every moment is precious, the foggy glasses become very clear. The priorities become simple and the journey less rocky.

Take a step back and allow the power of the now to help you focus on what is important.

365

NOVEMBER 17TH

I have made some mistakes in my life. I didn't always have what we would call the right answer. Would I change the past? Nope! You know why? Because the past doesn't define me, but it has shaped my present. I have learned from my mistakes and continue down my road called "growth." We grow and through growth we become the people we are today.

So yes, I made some mistakes, but I now have the ability to look at them from a different perspective. This new me will be better than ever.

365

NOVEMBER 18TH

I've got joy deep down in my soul. What could give you joy that feels that good? In most cases, it is something simple! A sunset, a walk by the lake, a smile or hug from that special someone.

It's usually the little things in life that bring us joy. Today you might be having a hard time finding or feeling that joy. It's there; you just got caught up in the noise. Break through the noise, turn down the volume, and get back to the joy. Take a moment to feel from within.

Never allow the noise to steal your joy!

365

NOVEMBER 19TH

Try walking into a crowded room and just taking the time to look around. Soak in your surroundings, listen in on a few conversations, watch people's facial expressions. You can take in and learn more by listening and observing. Sometimes it's best to say less!

You know the saying "What I would give to be a fly on the wall". Heard that one before? Well, it's true. Take some time to just listen. Learn through what you hear and what you see. You will be surprised where that experience might take you.

365

NOVEMBER 20ᵀᴴ

Take some time to thank your true friends. Through the good and bad times, your true friends are there. Through growth, you can distinguish between those who are true friends and those who are not.

A best friend has lived the stories with you and will walk with you through fire. They touch your heart because they look deep into your soul. Know your true friends and it will help you figure out the ones who are not.

Hebrews 13:2

Do not forget to show hospitality to strangers, for by so doing some people have shown hospitality to angels without knowing it.

NOVEMBER 21ST

Stepping into the unknown is never easy. The next chapter can be scary as hell. You have been in this situation before. Take the plunge and see what's on the other side.

They say, "You won't know until you try." Don't let fear, people, or just the unknown keep you from your blessing.

God has something special for all of us. As I've heard others say, "Step out on faith and let God lead the way."

POSITIVE THOUGHTS, POSITIVE VIBES!

365

NOVEMBER 22ND

The optimist sees the good, the opportunity and the green light in everything. The pessimist might be operating with a red light mentally, and always finds problems.

Our lives are comprised with a little bit of both. Not everything will be as beautiful as a bouquet of roses. There will be times when the thorns take over. Your outlook and perception is your choice. Try to see the good and beauty in most of the things you approach. Only you have the ability to stop you.

ANYTHING IS POSSIBLE
WITH THE RIGHT POINT OF VIEW.

NOVEMBER 23RD

Sometimes getting lost can help you find your way. Not knowing which way to turn can put you on the right path. They say, everything happens for a reason, and there is a time and place for everything.

Take a step back and let God lead. Allow Him to order your steps and He will guide you in the right direction.

Our way is not always the right way. Our plans might not be His plan for us. So you are not lost, my friend. He's just waiting for you to find Him.

365

NOVEMBER 24TH

Do you feel like you're spinning out of control? Feel like you're stuck in a tornado with life's debris flying around you? Like you're being pulled apart in every direction at once? Do you duck when the obstacles fly towards you instead of facing them head on?

When the world seems to be barreling down on you and you feel like you are spinning out of control, take a moment to stop and breathe. Allow your spirit to rest a little today.

NOVEMBER 25TH

Where you were, and are now, shapes the person you will be. Can you change the past? Maybe?

Growth allows us to look at things from a new perspective. A new point of view can provide a different outlook on things from your past. Sometimes you need to confront your past fears to move into the present.

You have the power to capture the moment that will help you move into the future.

POSITIVE THOUGHTS, POSITIVE VIBES!

365

NOVEMBER 26TH

Today and every day, we embrace gratitude
for the beautiful life we are blessed with and
the incredible people who enrich it.
Thanksgiving offers us a special moment to
pause and reflect on the abundance of
positivity surrounding us. It reminds us to
appreciate the gifts, big and small, that fill
our lives with meaning and joy. Whether it's
the love of family, the support of friends, or
the camaraderie of coworkers, this is the
perfect opportunity to come together, share
in gratitude, and celebrate the moments that
make life truly special. With hearts full of
thanks, may we continue to spread joy, love,
and positivity—today and always.

NOVEMBER 27ᵀᴴ

Nothing feels better than allowing your spirit to give. I believe some of the happiest people are the ones who give.

Offer a kind word, help a family in need, lend an ear when someone needs to be heard. You receive by allowing positive thoughts into your soul and by letting go of the negative ones.

Your spirit is open to receive the joy that is waiting for you. Giving comes in many forms; don't stress, just be!

NOVEMBER 28TH

Have I told you lately that I love being around you? The way you make me feel, make me laugh. I just enjoy being in your presence. Maybe it feels good having you in my life.

I love how we are able to sit and talk for hours. I love the positive energy that you exude that makes me feel so good. I can't wait to get together again so you can rejuvenate my mind, body and soul. Being in your presence makes me feel so good.

Today and every day, I wanna make sure you know; I just love the positive vibes you have brought into my life.

365

NOVEMBER 29TH

Our ability to connect is so important in our day-to-day living. That connection allows us to conduct business and establish friendships.

Through growth, we understand ourselves better which allows us to continue to build positive connections; dissolving the ones that tear us down.

The best connections let you be you, which will attract the best people to travel on your journey with you.

POSITIVE THOUGHTS, POSITIVE VIBES!

365

NOVEMBER 30TH

Here I go again, I am struggling to get to the gym. I know how important it is to exercise but I am really struggling. How do I get motivated? Should I just buy a size up in those jeans?

It's all about baby steps my friend. Rome wasn't built in a day. Don't move too fast or too slow. It's done at your own pace and maybe with a little assistance. Take a walk, hike or even a few sit-ups while watching your favorite show. You don't have to do it all at once. This is a marathon baby!

With the right mindset and a little support, you will start to create the change you want to see.

DECEMBER 1ST

NATIONAL PIE DAY

I can still taste the creaminess of my mother's sweet potato pie—my all-time favorite, right up there with a warm slice of apple pie topped with ice cream. National Pie Day is the perfect chance for all of us pie lovers to indulge in a slice of sweet, comforting goodness.

Whether it's apple pie, cherry pie, pecan pie, or, of course, my beloved sweet potato pie, let's savor each bite and maybe even share a piece with someone else.

365

DECEMBER 2ND

Do yourself a favor: surround yourself with people who ignite that same spark in you, and use it to propel yourself toward being the best person you can be.

It's true, the people around you, their attitude, the way they look at the world, their sour disposition and even their frustration can bleed onto you and bring your positive vibes down.

You don't have to unfriend them, just step away long enough to recharge and bring them some positivity later.

POSITIVE THOUGHTS, POSITIVE VIBES!

365

DECEMBER 3ᴿᴰ

You don't always have the capacity to handle it all and you don't need to. Yes, you can take on everyone else's problems and add them to yours. Superman or Superwoman, you wear the name quite well. It could be time to start living a more problem-free life.

Recharge yourself so your mind, body and soul are ready to accept what God has in store for you. It's ok to say, "No. Sorry, I'm busy," or, "I just can't deal with that right now." If you can push a few things aside, the positive energy will have room to enter. Trust me, that is a good thing.

365

DECEMBER 4TH

Let go of the past, and stare at the future. We all carry emotional baggage. You know, that stuff we carry around from the past that affects our present. It keeps us in the past while also pushing us into the future. Then what happens is, we forget about the NOW!

Trying to get out of the mess is not always easy, but it is necessary. When you forgive, you start to let go and unlock your spirit. A free spirit will allow you to move into the present and put some of that past behind you.

365

DECEMBER 5TH

We have to remember that we live in an imperfect world. There will always be something to worry about. Did you accomplish everything today? How can you solve that problem in your life? It's impossible for us to take care of everything and make sure everything is perfect.

Your objective is to give your best. Understand that some problems can't be solved. Some things are not yours to worry about. Don't allow your spirit to be consumed with the negativity of the world.

Worrying too much will not move you forward. It will take you off of your path of positivity.

365

DECEMBER 6TH

You know exactly what I'm talking about. That someone, your person or persons, that just makes you feel good. Being in their presence is what you've been longing for.

When you think of them, they make you smile, laugh, and provide a little bit of peace when needed. It's like pure joy being in their presence.

Minutes, hours, or even a few months can go by and the feeling never changes. They offer a safe space for you to "just be". Allowing your heart to be open and your soul to be filled. Hold on to the ones that fill your mind, body and soul with the peace you deserve.

DECEMBER 7ᵀᴴ

Kirk Franklin said it best, "Melodies from Heaven rain down on me." In the midst of the storm, ask God to pour himself all over you. Stand still and feel the freshness of the rain as it washes away your sorrows, fears and negative thoughts. You must let go and let God take control and get you through those tough times.

Listen to the song He has given you and dance that dance of rejoice. He will fill you up like you never have felt before.

Reference: *Line sung by* Kirk Franklin *in the song* "Melodies from Heaven" *Album* "Songs from the Storm, Volume 1*"2006*

365

DECEMBER 8TH

Feeling peaceful is not allowing negative thoughts or energy to take over. Surround yourself with inspiring people and positive things. Take some time to declutter your mind and allow your soul to feel at peace. What does the feeling of peace feel like?

Have the courage to change the things you can and understand the things you cannot. It is the ability to let go, and let God lead you. There are many things that will distract you from achieving some type of peace. Find a way to have less control and allow life to just be. Take time to breathe and be still. This will declutter your world and get you closer to achieving peace.

365

DECEMBER 9ᵀᴴ

You woke up this morning, so thank God for
the many blessings in your life.

Yes, we all have tough days but today is
your day to let go of the negativity.

But remember this, it is your journey, and
your blessings belong to you. Own it!

Put yesterday behind you
and move forward with today!

POSITIVE THOUGHTS, POSITIVE VIBES!

365

DECEMBER 10ᵀᴴ

I wander at times. The Spirit leads me to random places where I get to make meaningful connections with strangers. Sometimes these connections are for a moment, sometimes they are for a lifetime.

We know that every single connection has meaning and purpose. Allow people to come in and out of your lives, freely, for these connections offer growth, and through that growth you gain wisdom.

365

DECEMBER 11ᵀᴴ

You're reflecting on your past, thinking about the journey that brought you here. Perhaps you've spent a good part of your life feeling like you weren't living the life you envisioned—whether it was the wrong career path, an unfulfilling relationship, or simply taking time to find your way.

Today is a new beginning—a clean slate to move forward and create the life you truly desire. You may not have all the answers yet, but with the right mindset and by surrounding yourself with supportive people, you can uncover the tools and guidance you need along the way.

365

DECEMBER 12TH

What would you consider fair?
Why do we need fairness?

In life you will be treated in ways that you feel are unfair. This unfairness is actually our own perception of what we consider to be fair. How we respond is key!

Can you let it go? You have control of how something or someone makes you feel. Approach the situation with good energy and let go of the negativity surrounding the circumstance. This is the perfect opportunity to let your optimistic outlook shine through.

DECEMBER 13ᵀᴴ

If you are reading this, God gave you a second chance on life. You've been given the gift of the present. Don't allow things of the past to bring you down!

Now is your chance to put those things behind you and focus on the now. Think about the things you want to fine-tune about yourself and just do it.

You have a second chance to get it right!

GO GET YOURS!

POSITIVE THOUGHTS, POSITIVE VIBES!

365

DECEMBER 14TH

Most of us spend so much time trying to solve problems; our own problems as well as our friends' and family's problems. That's not what we are here for -- solving as many problems as possible. When you see or feel all of those problems coming your way, stop and breathe.

Understand that you are only one person and God only gives us 24 hours in a day. Sometimes it's ok to say, "No!" Make sure that you do your part in balancing your life first. This will allow you to pick the problems you are best able to tackle and the ones you don't need to.

365

DECEMBER 15TH

Life is not perfect, we've all seen our share of ups and downs. Life's challenges and experiences have shaped us into who we are today. I'm forever grateful for the many conversations I've had with you all. The stories you have shared inspire me to write about our day to day being.

Yes, we strive every day to be the best we can be. Some days are harder than others, but we push through. That's what it's all about, pushing through and moving forward. This Positive Vibes movement hopes to sprinkle in a little positivity along your journey. Together we each can keep encouraging and motivating the world!

365

DECEMBER 16TH

You don't have to do it all alone. Yes, there are some things that can be better done alone, but you can usually accomplish more as a team.

The ability to understand and work with others is so important. Collectively we can have a huge impact on creating change in the world.

One person can light the spark and it's up to the rest of us to keep the flame going. No matter if it's personal, professional, or community-related, reach out and encourage others to join you.

Two minds are more powerful than one.

DECEMBER 17TH

I can see us sitting there, holding hands, sipping on a drink, getting lost in the flames without the need to say a word. It's a beautiful unusual mild winter night, with a slight breeze in the air.

There is something about being outside in nature with the warmth of the fire. The sense of peace consumes us bringing about stillness. Allow for the moments to take hold of you and embrace the power they hold.

POSITIVE THOUGHTS, POSITIVE VIBES!

365

DECEMBER 18ᵀᴴ

Dreamers, keep on dreaming! Who said that your dreams are not possible?

Yes, we don't know the future but if we stay in the now we can understand ourselves. Grab what you know and start with that. The road will get hard and you might not know where to turn. Just pick up the pieces and reclaim what is yours.

Most successful people have stumbled a few times. So, stand up tall and don't allow anything or anyone to knock you down.

You've got this!

365

DECEMBER 19ᵀᴴ

How do you respect and love yourself?

People come into our lives all of the time. When we respect ourselves, we show them how we would like to be treated. When we love ourselves, our true selves will shine bright for the world to see.

It is up to us to understand that we're not here to be accepted by everyone. God made you in the form He wanted. Love and respect who that person is and look within.

365

DECEMBER 20TH

There will be times when we need to compromise for the common good. Should we compromise ourselves or just a situation or circumstance?

The ability to see the big picture can help guide your steps. Some might say, "Never sell yourself to the devil." Understand this is give and take; no one will get exactly what they want but maybe they'll get the chance to move forward.

Put the past behind and live in the now.

365

DECEMBER 21ST

Are you living a life that is true to you? God wants us to have heaven on earth. Is this possible? Of course, it is! Keep it simple and be YOU!

Your ability to understand who you are and what you have to offer should be your priority. Don't try to be someone others want you to be. Be a good person, give your best and love life.

Don't focus on the afterlife, but the present life. Don't judge, but love what you feel in the now. Control what you can and let go of what you cannot.

365

DECEMBER 22ND

The world we live in looks like a mess sometimes. Crime, poverty, drugs, war; every time you turn on the television it's bad news and they hardly ever showcase a good news story.

Our lives can also be a mess, having us spinning around like a spinning top. Sometimes it's best for us to be still and stop thinking about our problems.

A moment of peace might allow you to see the problem differently and provide a new approach. That approach might provide some peace in the midst of the struggle and hopefully let you rise above.

365

DECEMBER 23RD

How do we heal ourselves? At some point in our lives the road will get pretty rocky. The other side of the storm is a place of healing.

The healing process has already started working, you just need to recognize it and own it. The tough times we go through, will form and shape us in ways that sometimes we have no control over. Look for blessings, find the positive and allow healing to occur. You might just find out some cool things about yourself you had no idea were there.

365

DECEMBER 24TH

Sometimes people come into our lives at the right moment. It could be just that simple. It can be simple enough to enjoy the moment, to take what is given you and to allow it to be.

Over thinking and over analyzing can lead you off the pathway meant for you. This is your time to grow, love and share, what is being offered.

Everyone will play a role. The closing act is yours for the taking.

365

DECEMBER 25TH

This holiday season, may the spirit of Christmas fill your heart with joy, love, and gratitude. As we reflect on the year gone by, let's remember that the greatest gifts aren't always wrapped in paper, but are found in the moments we share and the connections we make.

Let this be a time to embrace the present, to cherish those around us and to spread kindness, hope, and positivity. May your heart be open to new possibilities, and may the joy of giving and receiving fill your days with peace and happiness. Wishing you a Merry Christmas and a year ahead full of growth, connection, and infinite potential!

365

DECEMBER 26<u>TH</u>

We all love getting gifts. What was the best gift you ever got? Was it something big or small? An article of clothing, nice card, new TV, flowers; the list goes on. The best gift may be spending some time with yourself.

Take some time to get to know you again. Taking time out to reconnect from within is a gift of inner peace. The feeling you get will help to cleanse and energize your soul.

There is no gift someone can give you that will feel better than connecting with yourself.

365

DECEMBER 27TH

I'm sitting here laughing at my attitude. I've allowed the world to pour all of its negativity on me, and my attitude is in the dumps. The best part about this is that I've recognized it, so it's up to me to create the change. Start with gratitude. Being grateful for all of the things that you have in your life. Take a moment to meditate. Go for a walk, clear your mind.

No matter what the world throws at us, we always have to remember we have control of ourselves. Sometimes changing the circumstances, situations, or just walking away for a second, can be the deciding factor in changing your attitude in a positive direction.

365

DECEMBER 28ᵀᴴ

I think the group, Boston, said it best, "don't look back". Today is a new day. The past is in the past, and a new day is breakin'. Yes, you feel great, refreshed, energized and on a new path. It's all about balance, step over those potholes, swerve around that road block and keep moving forward.

You haven't felt this good in a long time so embrace the new you. Nothing is gonna hold you down now because the present feels good and it's propelling you into the future. You're breathing new air so don't look back.

365

DECEMBER 29$^{\underline{TH}}$

As we close out this year, we reflect on the amazing achievements we've celebrated, as well as the challenges we've faced. Each year brings its own blend of highs and lows, offering us valuable opportunities for growth, learning, and reflection. As we step into the new year, let's commit to surrounding ourselves with positivity, embracing new perspectives, and extending grace to ourselves and others as we continue on the journey of becoming the best versions of ourselves. Thank you all for being part of the Positive Vibes movement—your support empowers us to inspire and uplift others, helping everyone stay focused on what truly matters.

365

DECEMBER 30ᵀᴴ

By surrounding ourselves with people who inspire, motivate, and challenge us to grow, we enhance our ability to evolve into the best version of ourselves. Remember, the more love, light, and positivity we pour into our own lives, the more of it we attract—creating a ripple effect that elevates both us and those around us.

Thank you all for your unwavering support, inspiration, and encouragement as we continue on this incredible journey of positive vibes. I'm so grateful for the relationships and connections I've built over the years.

365

DECEMBER 31ST

Did you forget that you are blessed? Just stand still and think of all the things you have. Food, shelter, a job, a sound mind, and the list goes on. Stop focusing on what you don't have and be thankful for what you do have.

Your perspective and perception could be the key to seeing the blessings in your life. As the song goes, "Every time I turn around, blessings on blessings." God wants you to have heaven on earth. He's giving you blessings. So, pause and accept what He has for you.

Song by Anthony Brown *and Group Therapy*

365

Philippians 4:8

*Finally, brothers and sisters,
whatever is true,
whatever is noble,
whatever is right,
whatever is pure,
whatever is lovely,
whatever is admirable
—if anything is excellent
or praiseworthy
—think about such things.*

ABOUT THE AUTHOR

Preston Mitchum Jr. has dedicated his life to giving back and making a difference. Born in Bronx, New York his family moved to Langley Park, MD in 1981.

His family established the Mitchum Lawn and Landscaping business shortly after. This is where his father, Mitchum Sr. worked for over 30 years, creating beautiful lawns and establishing relationships throughout the community.

Preston Jr. is a graduate of Towson State University where he took his love for video and became an 18-year veteran news photographer for WMAR-TV in Baltimore, Maryland.

During this time, he founded The PMJ Foundation to create change in the Baltimore community. The foundation's vision is to impact families through programs and services that offer positive growth. The foundation has served thousands throughout Maryland.

With the passing of his father, Preston has taken over the family business and will continue to provide the quality service that his family established for many years.

365

~

A portion of the proceeds of this book
will support the programs that the
PMJ Foundation offers.

~

This book is dedicated to Preston's
two wonderful sons, Carter and Harrison.

~

Preston hopes that the positive message this
book has to offer will impact thousands and
create positive vibes that we all can feel.

THE PMJ FOUNDATION

PRESENTING POSSIBILITIES
FOR BRIGHTER FUTURES

The PMJ Foundation's Career Awareness Project (CAP) after-school program brings the outside professional world into the classroom. Community volunteers share their careers with our participants, inspiring at-risk youth to explore the infinite possibilities of college and career opportunities.

~

To learn more about the PMJ Foundation please visit: **www.pmjfoundation.org**

365

ERIN GO BRAGH Publishing

Erin Go Bragh Publishing publishes various genres of books for numerous authors. Their portfolio consists of a 1200-page Vietnamese to English Dictionary, Historical fiction, an award-winning children's educational series, multiple adult novels and memoirs, tween adventure stories, as well as Christian Fiction. Their objective is to promote literacy and education through reading and writing.

www.ErinGoBraghPublishing.com
Canyon Lake, Texas

REFERENCES